WILD BOARS LIVE TWICE!

Thai Cave Rescue: Mission Impossible

Michael Lum Y.M.

ISBN 978-981-14-0234-0
Library of Congress Control Number: 2019900628

DEDICATED TO

Wild Boars Football Academy
Duganpet Promtep (Nickname: Dom), 13, captain cum striker.
Chanin Vibulrungruang (Nickname: Titan), 11, forward.
Sompong Jaiwong (Nickname: Pong), 13, left winger.
Peerapat Sompiangjai (Nickname: Night), 17, right winger.
Prajak Sutham (Nickname: Note), 14, midfielder.
Mongkol Booneiam (Nickname: Mark), 13, midfielder.
Pipat Pho (Nickname: Nick), 15, midfielder.
Panumas Saengdee (Nickname: Mig), 13, defender.
Nattawut Takamrong (Nickname: Tern), 14, defender.
Pornchai Kamluang (Nickname: Tee), 16, defender.
Adul Sam-on, 14, defender.
Ekarat Wongsukchan (Nickname: Bew), 14, goalkeeper.
Ekapol Chantawong (Nickname: Ake), 25, assistant coach.

IN MEMORY OF

Saman Gunan
Departed Friday July 6, 2018

PROLOGUE

"**R**aise your hands!"

"Thank you." A barely audible, but polite voice responded.

In pitch darkness, as he digging the wall with a stone, he heard some swishing sounds emitting from the water like hungry fish in a pond surfacing to grasp food pellets. Seconds later, a shimmering light source popped out of the water, followed by another. Two mysterious, blackish, underwater creatures made an appearance, protecting their turf, protesting the presence of intruders.

Adul was temporarily blinded.

Monday, July 2 2018, Tham Luang Cave, Chiang Rai Province, Northern Thailand.

"How many of you?" enquired John, with great concern.

"Thirteen," Adul replied weakly in deep appreciation, thanking the Lord above for answering his prayers. Limited supply of precious tears, like pearls, rolled down, moisturizing his dry and sunken cheeks.

"Thirteen?" John repeated, seeking to assure himself he heard correctly.

"Yeah, yeah." Adul confirmed positively in halting English.

"Brilliant!" John exclaimed, reveling in the joy of discovery.

Frantic fear earlier written all over the faces of twelve boys and one man were temporarily erased as a sliver of hope radiated from the two light sources, not unlike twin spotlights hovering precariously across a dark, dilapidated theatre of old.

In the shimmering light, the thirteen could view clearly, for the first time in nine days, the murky water that flowed vengefully from the monsoon rain into the dark recesses of the spooky cave. And the two heaven-sent saviors-in-black that emerged from the depths of the treacherous water.

This marked the end of a death-defying nine days that began with an innocuous excursion that went horribly wrong, and the beginning of a seemingly impossible four-day rescue mission laden with high risks. It was an ice-thin line of confluence with the Grim Reaper and his scythe on one side meeting face-to-face with the guardian angels of heaven on the other.

Who says miracles don't happen in life? Who says mission impossible cannot be transformed into mission possible? And who says God doesn't hear our prayers?

There was certainly light at the end of the tunnel, in this case, a dark, mysterious and spooky cavern. So near and yet so far...

And the seemingly impossible drama unfolds...

PART ONE

The Cave Excursion

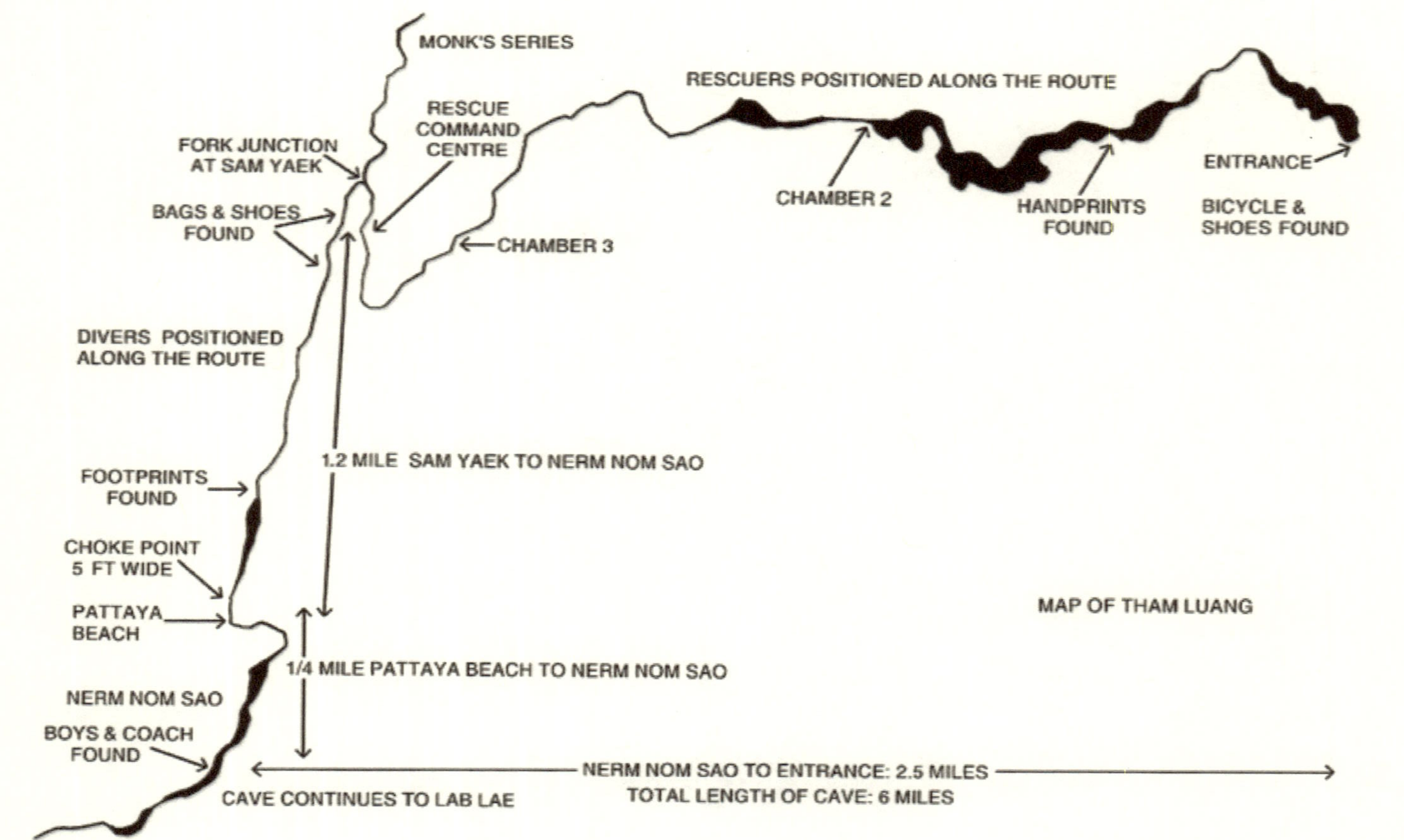
MONK'S SERIES
RESCUE COMMAND CENTRE
FORK JUNCTION AT SAM YAEK
BAGS & SHOES FOUND
CHAMBER 3
RESCUERS POSITIONED ALONG THE ROUTE
CHAMBER 2
HANDPRINTS FOUND
ENTRANCE
BICYCLE & SHOES FOUND
DIVERS POSITIONED ALONG THE ROUTE
1.2 MILE SAM YAEK TO NERM NOM SAO
FOOTPRINTS FOUND
CHOKE POINT 5 FT WIDE
PATTAYA BEACH
MAP OF THAM LUANG
1/4 MILE PATTAYA BEACH TO NERM NOM SAO
NERM NOM SAO
BOYS & COACH FOUND
CAVE CONTINUES TO LAB LAE
NERM NOM SAO TO ENTRANCE: 2.5 MILES
TOTAL LENGTH OF CAVE: 6 MILES

CHAPTER ONE

"Shoot!"

Ake, the assistant coach, yelled out to Pong, a 13-year-old left winger whose dream was to play for the Thai national team. He unleashed his right foot and ramped the ball towards the goal post. Pong was so football crazy that he invested all his spare time in either playing or watching the beautiful game.

The goal mouth was guarded by Bew, 14. Tall and lanky for his age, he was a natural choice to be the goalkeeper. Safeguarding between the posts, he repelled any intrusion into his sacred territory. His parents worked as shopkeepers.

The ball swiveled and rocked the goal post. It rebounded to Dom.

"Run faster. Down the wing!" Ake favored counter-attacking football. The strategy withdrew players into their own half except for one or two strikers. This would separate the strikers from the defenders. The strikers lurked around the halfway line, waiting to create space for a lightning-fast surprise attack.

Dom shot on sight. The ball took a curved path and shook the netting.

"GOAL!"

Dom, 13, was the captain and striker-in-chief of the team. At times mischievously boisterous, he was popular with the girls. He harbored a dream of being a professional footballer.

"It's really foggy. I can't see the ball coming in," complained Bew, the goalkeeper whose critical duty was akin to a spider spinning a web and preventing any insect from flying in.

Most Thai people, like these boys, have two names: a nickname and an official name. The nickname is chosen by the parents and given at birth before the official name has been registered. Nicknames can describe a baby's appearance or desirable characteristics like courage. In animism practice, babies are given two names to confuse malevolent spirits who may want to steal the baby. Calling a baby by an undesirable name, like "Pig" or "Fat", is believed to deter spirits from snatching him or her. For similar reasons, parents refrain from praising their baby.

A dozen boys, ranging from eleven to seventeen, were playing football in Ban Chong Sport Stadium. They were members of Mu Pa (Wild Boars in Thai) Football Academy. After their football practice, Ake usually continued leading his team on adventure tours, cycling and trekking through the forest park to strengthen both their physical endurance and mental resilience. While physical strength could be developed and measured, mental toughness was challenging. Cycling for fifty to sixty miles was the norm. Sometimes, they waded playfully in the waterfalls that disrupted the homogenous evergreen forest with a water element.

The Wild Boars were from a sleepy rural village in Mae Sai, a verdant countryside town. The village snuggled securely amidst the Doi Nang Non mountain range. A portion of the range is managed as the Tham Luang-Khun Nam Nang Non Forest Park.

Doi Nang Non is endowed with green virgin forest and sprinkled with Jurassic-like caves and picturesque waterfalls. When seen from certain angles, its silhouette bears an uncanny resemblance to a reclining woman with long hair. Its highest point, Doi Tung, is her belly. In many areas, coffee plantations have replaced opium farms. There is a standing joke (no pun intended) among its licensed guides to tourists: 'If this lady ever wakes up and stands on her feet, Doi Nang Non will be taller than Mount Everest.'

Can you see the silhouette of a sleeping lady with long hair?

Mae Sai lies 528 miles north of Bangkok. Mae Sai is the remote northernmost district of Chiang Rai province in northern Thailand. It is a major border crossing town between Thailand and Myanmar. Located in the heart of the Golden Triangle, it straddles between Thailand, Myanmar, China and Laos. The lawless triangular wilderness has the most extensive opium-farming fields in the world.

Thailand is located in the northern part of Southeast Asia. At 200 square miles, its size is between that of California and Texas. It has a population of sixty-eight million people, the population of California and Texas combined. Bangkok, its capital, has a population of ten million. It is world-renowned for its chili-hot tom yum soup, intricate temples with many imposing statues of Buddha and opulent royal palaces. On the nocturnal side, it is famous for its girly bars and traditional Thai massage that get your bones cracking.

Early Thais migrated from southwestern China. Known as people of The Land of Smiles, the Thais are friendly and courteous to the extent that they put both hands together in a prayerful mode to greet you. Thais are gentle people and they frown on raised voices.

Thailand is ruled by Prime Minister Prayut Chan-o-cha, previously an army general who took over from Yingluck Shinawatra in a 2014 coup. Yingluck is the younger sister of Thaksin Shinawatra, who served as Prime Minister from 2001 till 2006 when he was also overthrown by a military coup.

Thailand is known for its pristine water, idyllic topical beaches, emerald green lagoons and Jurassic limestone caves. James Bond movies like *Tomorrow Never Dies*, starring Pierce Brosnan, and *The Man with the Golden Gun*, starring Roger Moore were shot in Phang Nga Bay. Leonardo DiCaprio acted on Koh Phi Phi island for the film, *The Beach*.

Unlike the West which has four seasons, Thailand has only three - hot, wet, and cool. From March to June, it is scorching. The wet season lasts from June till October. It has the characteristics of heavy monsoon downpour and rough seas. The heavens open and it rains cats and dogs.

Flash flooding is common.

"Faster!"

"To your left!"

Ake shouted as he pointed his fingers at Tern, 14, a defender, who was already running for his life as if a German Shepherd was chasing him. He attended the nearby Mae Sai Prasitsart school together with six other teammates.

The boys, like many others in Asia, enjoyed kicking a ball around in whatever open grass patches that were available. With investments in just a hand-me-down ball, boots and pirated jerseys of popular clubs, football presented an affordable sport that lasted for two hours. It was a pastime in which many Thai boys indulged in the quaint sleepy town crisscrossed with clay paths and surrounded by lush green mountains, something that is a rarity in this digital world. Ake and his brood of twelve boys were no different. Every other day, except for heavy downpours, the boys gathered in this overused field and spent the otherwise lazy afternoon honing their skills.

The game began with some warm up. Stretching their hands upwards into the sky and reversing onto the ground, swinging their arms to the extreme right and left alternately, and jumping and hopping for a short distance. This all took about twenty minutes. It was capped off by jogging slowly around the perimeters before playing a game of forty-five minutes for each half, with a fifteen-minute break.

Shirtless children with their innocent looks, loitered by the sidelines to watch the match and pass their time. Sometimes, mothers were present, cuddling their year-old babies in their cotton harness to enjoy both the game and the afternoon breeze. When the sun retired and called it a day, parents would know precisely where to locate the children if they were not back home for dinner.

When the game finished, Ake gathered the boys to sit down in a campfire-like circle and he debriefed with them. He singled out mistakes and suggested how they could improve in future.

"You must kick the ball out of the line immediately, every time you sense danger," Ake advised Adul, a defender, during the debrief.

"Yes, *Pee* Ake," Adul acknowledged obediently. *Pee* is Thai for elder brother and a term that shows respect for seniority.

Ake, 25, was the assistant coach to the football team. He was born a Tai Lue, an ethnic minority in Shan State in Myanmar. At the tender age of ten, his parents and younger brother suffered and later died of a disease, leaving him an orphan. For two years, he was cared for by extended family. His aunt, Umporn, portrayed him as a sad and lonely boy. At twelve, he was packed off to become a monk's apprentice at the Wat Phra That Doi Wao monastery in Chiang Rai province. Monks pledged vows of silence, poverty and celibacy.

After ten years, Ake left monkhood to care for his sick grandmother. During this time, he was hired to be the assistant coach of Mu Pa Football Academy. A devout Buddhist, Ake meditated daily. He balanced his religious life with trekking and other outdoor activities in his free time. Ake empathized and bonded with the boys well, especially some of them who were stateless like him.

Parents of the football players also called Ake '*Pee* Ake' respectfully as he was the assistant coach to their sons, anyhow. Ake still maintained contact with the monastery. Its abbot singled him out as a responsible young man who meditated regularly.

Adul,14, the eldest of five children, was born in Wa state, a self-governing tribe in Myanmar that is not recognized internationally. In its earlier days, it practiced headhunting. Wa state is known for opium farming, methamphetamine trafficking and guerrilla warfare. At the age of six, Adul's parents smuggled him across the border into Mai Sai so he could have a better shot at education; otherwise, he would have been conscripted as a child soldier to guard opium farms. He would have grown up to be an illiterate and impoverished man. Adul was accepted by a local Baptist church where thirty to thirty-five children between the ages of six to fourteen could study in one class. An all-rounder, Adul topped the class and excelled in sports in Ban Wiang Phan School. With a flair for languages, he could speak five: English, Thai, Mandarin, Burmese and Wa. Adul also played three musical instruments.

Besides playing football, Adul was also kinesthetically gifted as a volleyball player. His team came in second in Northern Thailand two years in a row. In recognition of his achievement, he was handed a scholarship that offered full tuition and meals in school. Among the Wild Boars, Adul was the best in school and in English. Only Adul and Bew, the goalkeeper, spoke English.

His school principal, Punnawit Thepsurin praised Adul, "Stateless children like him have a fighting spirit that makes them want to excel." School director Phunawhit Thepsurin described Adul as a gem.

Mark was a cheerful and friendly boy. He was in the same volleyball team as Adul. Originally from Myanmar, Mark and his mother also migrated to Thailand.

Ake, Adul, Mark and Tee are among the half a million who are stateless, i.e. they are not recognized as citizens of any country. Because of travel restrictions, they cannot travel beyond Chiang Rai for away games nor become professional footballers. Even children that are born and raised in Thailand can still be stateless. To qualify for citizenship, the child must be born in Thailand, and additionally, the parents must belong to a recognized ethnic group and have lived in the country for several years.

Adul was one of these self-made boys.

The fault lies not in our stars.

CHAPTER TWO

"Bend!"

"Bend to your right. Go as far down as possible. Good."

"Bend to your left. Go down, go down."

"Now bend to your right again," instructed Ake.

It was Friday, June 22, 2018, Ban Chong Sports Stadium, Chiang Rai, Northern Thailand.

The boys, like the biblical Twelve Apostles, listened and obeyed religiously. Their big dream was to become professional footballers not unlike those you see in the English Premier League, Spanish La Liga and German Bundesliga. Football is big business in Asia. Thais are fanatics about football. According to FIFA, Thailand is ranked 122. In Asia, Thailand ranks ninth with Australia, South Korea and Japan in the top three.

Popular European football clubs include Liverpool, Manchester United, Arsenal, Barcelona, Real Madrid, Juventus and Bayern Munich. The previous Thai prime minister, Thaksin Shinawatra once owned Manchester City but later sold it to Sheikh Mansour of Abu Dhabi in 2008. Another club admired by the Thais is Leicester

City owned by Vichai Srivaddhanaprabha, founder-owner of King Power Duty, who died in a helicopter crash in October 2018. Dubbed as The Unbelievables, they won the 2015–16 English Premier League miraculously.

Ake innovated a system where the boys' passion for football would fuel their desire to excel in school, too. If they attained certain grades, they would be rewarded with football accessories like apparel or fresh studs. Both Ake and his boss, the chief coach, Nopparat Kanthavong, 37 years old, invested time diligently scouting for sponsors. They wanted to prove a point – boys from a small town could transform into professional footballers.

A non-smoker and a teetotaler, Ake looked after himself well. He imparted the same set of values to the boys. Totally dedicated to them, he treated the boys as if they were his own – ferrying them to and fro. They were put on a regimented training schedule that included cycling in the hills.

When the game ended, Ake gave the boys valuable feedback.

"That concludes our training today. It will pump you up for the match tomorrow where you all can prove your worth. After that, you will be initiated," said Ake.

"What is that?" queried Mig, an agile player in defense. At thirteen, he had a bigger frame than his peers which suited his role as a stout defender.

"Initiation is a special ceremony to mark your acceptance into our promising football club."

"Wow. That's cool!" exclaimed Mark in awe.

"Where are we having our initiation?" asked Note curiously. A fast learner and brilliant boy, he babysat his two-year-old sister whenever he was at home.

"The cave!" yelled some of the boys in unison. They were raring each another to go. They have also discussed about the cave in their facebook group. At an impressionably tender age, the boys were curious to know just about everything, including the cave. It was as normal for these rural boys in Chiang Rai and Cheng Mai to explore caves as it was for boys in Bangkok to visit shopping malls.

"We've not been inside the cave before. We want to see how is it like!" echoed some boys. The boys usually passed this tourist attraction on the way to football practices. 1,500 to 2,000 tourists visited the cave per day. On the weekends, the numbers swelled to 3,000 to 4,000 per day. At the entrance, there were stories promoting attractions at different spots of the cave - The Planetarium, Maze City, Stalactite Cave, Underwater City and The Hidden City. It piqued the boys' interest.

"It's my first time. Let's go for it. Outside school, I want to get a new experience in my life," reasoned Adul.

Having a soft spot for them, an empathic Ake accommodated their wishes, although he and two other boys had been there before. He was a believer that outdoor activities such as hiking in the cave stretched his charges' mental limits while adding agility to their game. Besides, team outings were fun and they forged *esprit de corps*.

"Tomorrow is Night's birthday. We can celebrate it in the cave," suggested Dom.

"Next Sunday, July first is Note's sixteenth birthday too," added Nick.

Chiang Rai, in Northern Thailand, is renowned for its queer caves – Wat Tham Pla (Fish Cave or Monkey Temple), Tham Phra (Buddhist Cave), Tham Luang Nang Non (Great Cave of the Sleeping Lady) and Chiang Dao. Inside some of the caves are shrines with an assortment of Buddha statues. They are revered as holy places where deities live.

"I need to be at home by five though," stated Night, 17, a right winger with a quiet disposition. Besides football, he was also a devoted member of a cycling club, Sittthisak Sawanrak.

"Not a problem. We'll be at the cave for only an hour," assured Ake.

"*Ainoo*, let's play at the stadium before going to explore the cave," announced Ake, confirming the schedule for the next day." *Ainoo* ("cute little mice" in Thai) was the boys' nickname.

As the boys were keen cyclists, Ake suggested they cycled to the stadium, the next morning on their Facebook group. They also communicated with the parents on this chatgroup.

That night saw the World Cup match between Brazil and Costa Rica. It was heading for a boring draw which was not surprising, considering the previous night's match where Croatia hammered Argentina, a previous world champion, 3-0. Miraculously, in injury time, Brazil sprang to life. Coutinho and Neymar scored one goal each within eight minutes of each another. The boys were delighted as Brazil was the most successful football team in history. She won the World Cup five times. Besides Germany, France and Spain, Brazil was another favorite to win the prestigious solid gold trophy depicting two human figures holding up planet Earth.

⇌ ⇋

"I'm back!"

"*Mae*, I'm back."

"Where are you, Mae?" Titan searched for his mother.

Friday, June 22, 2018, a village in Mae Sai, Chiang Rai, Northern Thailand.

Titan, 11, the baby of the Mu Pa Football Academy. He played in the frontline as a deadly shoot-on-sight striker. At the young age of seven, he started kicking a football around before joining his school's sports club. Later, the Wild Boars sent him a personal invite to join them.

"How was the training, *look chaai*?" the mother asked her son, using an endearing term common amongst Thai families.

"Fantastic. We're going to the cave tomorrow after our practice."

"Shall I cook *Khao Niaw* with *Sai Oua*? I can pack them in a lunch-box for you."

Khao Niaw is sticky rice. The famous *Sai Oua* sausage, also known as Chiang Mai sausage, is a knockout recipe handed down from grandmothers, consisting of spiced pork sausage, seasoned with lemongrass and kaffir lime leaves, among other ingredients.

"No thanks, *Mae*. We're there for only an hour," Titan thanked her respectfully. Thai families are close-knit. Children obeyed their elders and practiced filial piety as preached by Buddhist philosophy.

"Alright. I'll prepare them for our dinner. Remember when you visit the cave, you must respect the customs. Caves have existed for thousands of years and there are many superstitions. Visitors must seek permission from the deities who guard them. If no permission is sought, they have to remain silent inside. Avoid profanity or openly criticizing any structure, items or animals found inside, however much you dislike them. A popular and wise Thai saying goes, 'Even if you don't believe, don't disrespect it.'

Remember also not to take anything from the cave, not even a small pebble or a sachet of soil as a souvenir. They form the whole ecological system that has existed for thousands of years. Spirits can dwell even in a small stone. Deities guard the cave and they lay a curse on the petty thief who removes an item from its original home."

Caves in Thailand hold a special kind of mystic power. This is why ascetic monks and hermits meditate in caves. That is also why there are shrines and offerings within the caves.

Across the village was Adul's humble abode. He was the only Christian in the Wild Boars football team. While studying in the local Baptist church, he embraced the faith. Thanks to the church education and missionary teachers, Adul could converse in five languages.

A straight-A student, Adul's ambition was be a doctor and a famous professional football player for Chiang Rai United. He admitted to one of his best friends, Luea-Boon Junta, "Football is my life."

"*Por*, there's a match between Nigeria and Iceland tonight," Adul informed his father. *Por* is Thai for father.

"Let's watch it together," proposed *Por*.

Father and son spent the night bonding at home by watching the World Cup.

Nigeria saw Iceland off at 2-0.

"Don't you dare!"

"Don't you dare go to the cave!"

Warangkana, 14, Tee's girlfriend issued him a warning. A girl's dare means not to do it at all costs, otherwise you will be a dead duck soon. Her uncanny prescience was evident in her deep frowns.

"Why not, *nong*?" challenged Tee, 16, the stout defender. *Nong* means younger brother or sister in Thai.

"*Pee* Tee, the weather is unpredictable. It can rain anytime!" the ominous answer came screaming.

"We play as a team. Every player is going. If I'm absent, one piece of the jigsaw puzzle is missing. I cannot let them down just because of you," Tee tried to clarify although he was usually a boy of a few words.

"Fine!" came the abrupt response.

When a girl exclaimed "Fine!", it was her way of finishing off an argument before all hell breaks loose.

And the line went dead. Tee used his phone to check the World Cup results: Serbia 1, Switzerland 2.

Besides Tee, Mig, a defender and Nick, a midfielder, also had girlfriends.

CHAPTER THREE

Cock-a-doodle-do!

Saturday, June 23, 2018 was the beginning of another week-end just like any other. As the rooster crowed to signal the break of dawn, the sun peeped shyly out of the foggy morning at 5.40 am. The temperature was slightly hot at 75 degrees Fahrenheit. Humidity was 97% and visibility was restricted to 3 miles. A mild wind was blowing at four miles per hour.

On this day, White House press secretary Sarah Sanders was unceremoniously kicked out of Red Hen, a Virginia farm-to-table fine dining restaurant, by its owner, Stephanie Wilkinson, because she worked for President Donald Trump.

Entrepreneurs seized the opportunity to cash in with T-shirts emblazoned with the phrase "I Really Do Care, Do U?", touting a social message. It was in response to the olive-green Zara jacket "I Really Don't Care, Do U?" that First Lady Melania Trump wore to visit migrant children at the Texas-Mexico border earlier in the week. The T-shirts were emblazoned with the same white graffiti-style font as Trump's.

The month of June 2018 hosted two major world events. On Tuesday, June 12, President Donald Trump met Kim Jong-un in Singapore for the first Peace Summit between the leaders of US and North Korea. On Thursday, June 14, the World Cup, held once in four years, kicked off in Russia. The opening match saw the host beat Saudi Arabia 5-0. Father's Day was celebrated on the third Sunday of June. The darker side of June saw two American celebrities take their own lives by hanging themselves in the same week. First was fashion designer, Kate Spade, who built a handbag empire. Three days later, celebrity chef Anthony Bourdain, who promoted international cuisine, departed. Both suffered from clinical depression.

It was just another mundane day except it was Night's birthday. Night had grown into a dashing young man at 16. By Thai custom, Night was 17 years old. Increasing a person's age by one year is a practice that originated in ancient China. When babies are born, they assume the age of one instead of zero. It is widely practiced by other cultures in East Asia too such as Vietnam, Korea and Japan.

Night's house located in Vieng Hom Village was a convenient meet-up point. Nearly every day, except in inclement weather, four of Night's football friends assembled at his house. As soon as all arrived, they would depart to play football. About a year back, Night had joined Wild Boars as a right winger. A quiet and polite boy, he was a person of brevity.

Night's family prepared a dinner with grilled pork and dessert. They would celebrate his birthday together with some relatives. Phunphatsa, Night's sister, bought a SpongeBob SquarePants birthday cake and hid it in the refrigerator to spring a pleasant surprise.

Night, the eldest of the team of players, simply adored SpongeBob SquarePants, an optimistic cartoon sea sponge who resembled a rectangular yellow kitchen sponge.

"Remember to come back early for your birthday dinner tonight, *nong chaai*" reminded Phunphatsa, addressing her younger brother with an endearing Thai word. Frequently, she assumed the role of a motherly figure to him.

"Thanks *Pee Saao*. I'll be back right on the dot," Night reassured her. *Pee Saao* is a respectful term for elder sister in Thai.

In the morning, at 84 degrees Fahrenheit, under a foggy sky, the boys departed the house for football practice. On the way, they stopped by a mom-and-pop shop housed in a hut constructed with rough wood and a zinc roof. They chipped in twenty-two dollars, a princely sum in this impoverished village, to purchase some cans of carbonated drink and an assortment of snacks to celebrate Night's birthday in the cave. The middle-aged husband and wife operators collected the money and wished them ominously,

"Stay safe!"

In the morning, Nopparat, the head coach, had an appointment elsewhere. He delegated his duties to Ake, his assistant, offering him the opportunity to coach the boys by himself.

He instructed, "Ake to take the boys for training at Ban Chong Sports Stadium. Make sure you ride your bicycle behind them when you are travelling around, so you can keep a lookout. Take care."

Ake responded dutifully, "Sure, boss."

Nopparat wished his assistant, "Do a good job, Ake."

"Sorry."

"Sorry, boys. The match is cancelled," Ake announced.

"But why?" asked Mark.

"They called me to cancel the match due to things beyond their control. Let's warm up before we go to explore the cave."

After a sweaty session, the boys rested and welcomed a faint breeze. Ake reviewed their strengths and mistakes committed unknowingly. At high noon, 88 degrees Fahrenheit, under an overcast gloomy sky, the job was done.

The mother of Songpol, 13, arrived to pick him up after training. All, except Songpol, rode their bicycles to the cave. On the way, they stopped at their favorite drinks stall.

"*Ainoo*, please place your orders," instructed Ake.

"*Cha Yen* again?" asked Kalayanin, a 46-year-old drink seller. *Cha Yen* is a popular milky iced tea. She always admired how Ake acted as a father figure to the boys.

They cycled leisurely through rice paddy fields and the mud paths and towards the cave burrowed in the mountains. As in life, it was not a smooth, straight path. At times, the ride was bumpy. They meandered through the paddy fields, the bush land, boulders and potholes. Silhouettes of buffaloes in the watery terraced fields presented a good photograph opportunity. From afar, they could see Doi Nang Non mountain where the cave was burrowed. Its outline was a lady with long hair lying down.

CHAPTER FOUR

"We're here!"

Friday, June 23, 2018, Tham Luang.

The tranquility surrounds of the cave greeted as the boys announced their arrival. The boys quickly parked their trusty bicycles against a railing made of two parallel wooden poles held together by vertical poles at regular intervals. Mountain bikes were transport workhorses in this rugged part of Northern Thailand. The white mountain bike stood up conspicuously. The rest were red, blue and black. Throwing caution to the wind, they flung their backpacks, football shoes and shin guards aimlessly on the ground. Each boy was armed with a cheap flashlight and spare batteries. One had a mobile phone while coach Ake wore a black SKMEI military watch and carried ropes.

One of the boys wore the red Three Lions jersey. Most of the boys supported England in the World Cup. Harry Kane was the striker and captain of the English team. Kane, who played for Tottenham Hotspurs, scored six goals and won the Golden Boot award for the most goals scored. Another boy wore a Real Madrid jersey.

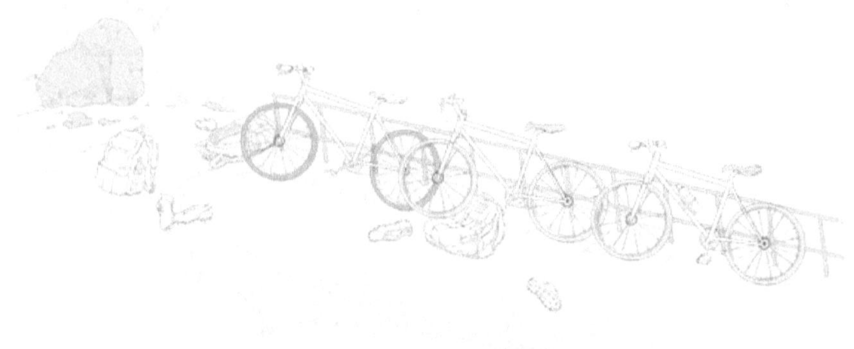

The boys parked their bicycles outside Tham Luang

The entrance of Tham Luang (Tham is Cave; Luang is Great in Thai) is like a giant mouth yawning. Weak rays of sunlight, filtering through the tree leaves, beamed into the cave mouth, giving it relief from dampness. A weak breeze attempted to refresh the slightly earthy smell emitted from within. Around the cave was verdant vegetation interspersed with grey and white rock formations. The sun was at its peak. This was a serene Saturday afternoon at Tham Luang.

Tham Luang Khun Nam Nang Non is a complex cave located in jungle-draped Tham Luang-Khun Nam Nang Non Forest Park, near the idyllic village of Pong Pha, in northern Thailand. The karstic cave is found beneath Doi Nang Non, a cloud-swathed mountain range, about two miles from the border shared with Myanmar.

The entrance of the cave is 66 feet long. It meanders and twists six miles deep into its belly northwards and then turns west in a long tunnel without many chambers. Its narrowest tunnel measures five feet wide. It has many deep recesses, grottos, narrow tunnels and sumps. Throughout the entire cave, breathtaking glittering stalactites and stalagmites are found in abundance. Many underground streams run here, some of them active throughout the year. During the monsoon season, an underground river flows through the cave. During the dry season, visitors can walk through the cave like an underworld city. After all, the Great Cave is the fourth largest cave in Thailand. Phu Pha Phet (Diamond Mountain) Cave is the largest in Thailand.

Tham Luang is spectacular. Visitors, young and old alike, are overwhelmed by the sheer size of its entrance that resembled a Gothic cathedral in Europe and its complex twisted caverns within. Here lies the perils of this formidable cave - within minutes, it can transform itself from an inviting and tranquil cave where you can meditate and connect with the universe, to a ruthless man-eating monstrous flood. From July to October, the southwest monsoon that arrives from India brings in heavy downpours.

<u>Tham Luang Legend</u>
Asia, with its 5,000 years of rich history, is steeped in legends and superstitions. Tham Luang Khun Nam Nang Non, the full name of the cave, is no exception. Translated literally, the Thai name means "the great cave and water source of the sleeping lady mountain."

Local Thais believe this sleeping lady was a beautiful, porcelain-skinned princess in Chiang Roong, Xishuangbanna (or Sip Song Panna), located between Mynamar, Laos and China. Long, long, ago, a princess went to the royal stable to take her favorite horse for a morning ride in the rolling hills. She met a simple but charming stable hand in the royal stable.

A stable hand or a groom is a person responsible for the management of horses and the stables. Besides cleaning the stables, he feeds, exercises and grooms horses. He is on call all the time in case any member of the royal household wishes to take the horses for a ride.

Eyes met. It was love at first sight. The beautiful, royal princess fell head over heels for a mere mortal. Soon, she was pregnant with their love child. The king was furious and forbade their marriage. The star-crossed lovers eloped to the mountains, pursued by the king's soldiers. Half way through the escape, the forbidden lovers stumbled upon Tham Luang Nang Non. They entered and found it a safe place to hide.

Meanwhile, the furious king ordered his soldiers to find the stable hand, dead or alive. When the stable hand emerged from the cave to hunt for food in the forest, the soldiers found and killed him. Overcome with grief, the princess stabbed herself with her hair pin. It penetrated precisely into her heart. She bled to death. The Doi Nang Non mountain, resembling a lying lady with long black hair, is the body of the princess. The cave is her bowels. The highest point in the mountain, Doi Tung, is her pregnant belly. Her head is Doi Chong or Doi Tha while Doi Mae Ya is her pair of breasts. The water that flows in the cave is her royal blood which forms the upstream of Mae Sai River.

The outline of Doi Tung mountain resembles the princess lying down

The Doi Tung mountain is mainly limestone and granite. Below 3,000 feet is mostly deciduous forest and above it is evergreen. Since year 911, it has been an important pilgrimage spot for the devout Buddhist. Doi Chong is a beautiful mountain with breathtaking views. It is a sanctuary for the near-extinct mountain goats and rare birds.

Till this day, the princess' spirit wanders to and from the mouth of the cave to the inner dark labyrinth stretching to six miles within. Her spirit guards its entrance to check if visitors are friends or foe. Should you enter the cave, beware what flows out of your mouth. Do not insult or degrade the princess, at all costs or at any time, lest supernatural mishaps occur when she is upset. Guard your mouth and be respectful. The sinister-looking walls of Tham Luang may be dead silent, but they do have ears.

Till this day, local Thais kneel and pray with hands clasped and head bowed to this young princess, Jao Mae Nang Non (The Reclining Goddess in Thai) in remote grottos or make-shift shrines. Prayers are answered for those who faithfully believe in her spiritual powers.

There are so many legends about spirits in caves. Now, the boys were more frightened than aware.

Maybe there was one lurking behind them ...

The Entrance
"1, 2, 3, 4, 5, 6, 7, 8, 9, 10, 11 … 12."

Ake instructed with a firm voice to reconfirm there were twelve boys in tow. It is a standard safety guideline any instructor worth his salt was expected to do - a headcount at regular intervals for outdoor activities.

"13." concluded Ake.

With every boy accounted for, the journey began.

The number "thirteen" has been long considered an unlucky number by many cultures. At the last supper, there were thirteen people around the table - Christ and the twelve apostles. One of those thirteen, Judas Iscariot, betrayed Jesus Christ. And if day "thirteen" falls on a Friday, westerners avoid it at all costs.

"Our journey starts now. We'll be here for only an hour, *Ainoo*," Ake budgeted his time. Before arrival, they had a full meal. So, they left most of their food and water on their bicycles.

"I'm excited," exclaimed Titan.

Before the entrance was a shrine of the princess, Jao Mae Nang Non. There were six life size statues of the lovely princess, each dressed in traditional Thai costume of different colors and garlanded with flowers. There were half burnt candles and joss sticks. On the altar were overflowed wax and ashes. There were fruit and chicken offerings. Thais prayed to the statues to appease the spirits of the cave.

Statues of The Reclining Goddess in shrines outside Tham Luang

In the early afternoon, scattered clouds were seen in the sky. The temperature rose to 86 degrees Fahrenheit. Ake and his team descended the height of two stories before they reached the cave.

As Ake and his twelve boys stood at the entrance of Tham Luang, they felt invincible, ready to conquer the formidable cave, admire its grandeur and face the unknown. Who could have carved such a gigantic opening? Were crates of treasures buried in the deep recesses? Was a female ghost in a long white gown and blood dripping from her eyes lurking in the labyrinth?

The entrance was where the surface met the underground environment. As there was sufficient sunlight, grass and trees flourished. Some bushes and trees even grew impossibly out of the rocks on either side of the entrance. It was cool and shaded. A large warning sign, screaming in red, was erected at a prominent position:

DANGER!

FROM JULY-NOVEMBER

THE CAVE IS FLOODED.

NO ENTRY

FROM HERE ON, NO ENTRY

The signboard was casting cursory glances on Ake but he chose to brush it off in this dry season.

This was not the first time Ake and two of the boys had explored Tham Luang. The challenge now was to explore deeper into the unknown and view new limestone formations. Perhaps, they would discover a new underground river, lake or waterfall or another exit.

The cave was not without its dangers. Cavers had gotten lost before although they were not first-time cave explorers. As the boys trekked, their adrenaline pumped up as if they were in a roller-coaster slowly inching its way to its peak before unleashing the full gravitational force.

The interior of the cave varies from the outside. Within the cave, the climate is relatively stable for the entire year. Due to the extremely low evaporation rates, the humidity is as high as 95%. Because of limited biodiversity, flora and sunshine, there is a scarcity of food resources inside the cave.

The paths, especially the first 400 feet, were worn out by the many curious tourists who arrived by the busloads but dared not venture beyond. Many locals, however, came here to pray. The walls were black, brown and grey. It was amazing how the forces of nature could carve such an awesome cathedral-like cavity in the depths of the mountain over thousands of years. It was incredible that the limestone cave could maintain its structure without collapsing under the weight of the mountain above. It was fascinating how a passage could worm itself deep inside for miles.

Some boys took off their sandals and walked barefooted. As they trekked, they teased each other and laughed. The air was damper now. A wave of eeriness hung surreptitiously over the air.

"I'm a bit scared," confessed Titan, the baby of the Wild Boars.

"It's getting darker and darker," confessed Dom, "My girlfriend teases me because I'm actually afraid of the dark. I guess this is the perfect exercise for me to get rid of my irrational fear. It's a good start. There's power in numbers. I feel braver in a team."

A voice from one of the boys mischievously proclaimed with a haunting voice,

"Let not the dark swallow you!"

CHAPTER FIVE

"Look, what is the place?" asked Bew.

"Sam Yaek," replied Ake.

After trekking for one and a half miles, the thirteen arrived at a fork-junction. Resembling a U-shaped fork pointing south, it offered two ways for cavers to proceed. Turning right led to another cave complex – Monk's Series. Turning left brought one to Pattaya Beach. As it is in life, you are presented with two options at the crossroad. They turned left.

The boys redirected the flashlights. Before their very eyes, unfolding before them, they witnessed, imposing stalagmite and stalagmites.

"Spooky!"

The eeriness gave some of the boys goosebumps.

"Stay calm, *ainoo*. There're thirteen of us," assured Ake. Their unity was strength. They descended another two to three stories down into the cave.

With weaker flashlights in their hands, the troop proceeded to explore the intricate dark bowels of the mountain, not unlike the intestines of a body. In the name of camaraderie and adventure, they ventured deeper, to a place some of them had never set foot on before.

"*Ainoo*, today is your special day. You'll be initiated in a unique ceremony," announced Ake.

"What is initiation, *Pee* Ake?" asked Mig.

Their fierce loyalty to the club and brotherhood of boys was, as if, cast in stone. To celebrate this landmark event of great significance, they needed to display their badge of courage and honor. The boys had to go through the rite of passage – crawling through the most dangerous and narrowest tunnel in Tham Luang – five feet wide. It was just wide enough for a person, head facing upward, to slide through with military precision. There was no margin for error.

"The purpose of this initiation is to eradicate your fears and push your limits. Confront your fears and do the things that you fear most. Once you've crossed fear, you will tread on new ground and achieve greater heights," Ake motivated them.

"This exploration in the dark across dangerous and tight passages also promotes teamwork where you help each other. It will be perfect if we can also apply it to our football matches. To conclude Wild Boars initiation, we will scrawl our names on the wall," ended Ake on a positive note.

The boys struggled precariously through the five feet-wide narrow passageway paved with sharp rocks. Like worms, the initiates wriggled up the passageway and down it at an inverted U-shaped choke point. There was hardly any space between the boys and the tunnel walls.

Emerging through the tunnels, the dozen was initiated; no longer novices. They felt they were no longer boys, but men.

"We've been here before."

They landed at Pattaya Beach where Ake and two of the boys came before.

Pattaya Beach was named after Pattaya, the city on the east coast of the Gulf of Thailand, about 62 miles south-east of Bangkok.

The actual Pattaya Beach is a three-mile crescent-shaped, idyllic sea-side resort. It is a festive and colorful hive of beach activities, diving boats and floating restaurants. It is famed for hostess bars, go-go bars, massage parlors, saunas, and hotels where lovers pay by the hour. Above all, Pattaya is world-renowned for its ladyboys.

The twelve plus one arrived at Nern Nom Sao which was about two and a half miles from the cave entrance.

"Should we continue to Lab Lae?" asked Ake of his charges to exercise a joint decision.

"How long will it take?"

"About an hour," answered Ake.

"I need to be home by seven. My family is celebrating my birthday," reminded Night.

"In that case, we'll call this our final destination for today. Congratulations for making it thus far. We'll make our way back now," instructed Ake.

They whistled happily on their return journey towards Pattaya Beach and the fork junction at Sam Yaek.

CHAPTER SIX

Swoosh!

Approaching the fork-junction at Sam Yaek in the afternoon, they heard a swooshing sound. An eerie, rushing sound. What was it?

Everyone remained silent as the sound grew louder. It seemed to approach nearer and nearer. The boys shone their flashlight on the ground in the direction of the sound.

It was the gushing sound of water. Water like café latte quickly invaded the dry bed of the path like spilled coffee swiftly engulfing a dry carpet. The uninvited guest rushed in and twirled in style, making its presence felt. The rate of water flowing in was faster than the rate of absorption by the ground. Soon, it overfilled the dry, low-lying areas and rose rapidly. The water brought along other unfriendly company – stones, sand and mud. It blocked the escape route entirely. The boys routed like a troop of defeated soldiers by quickly swimming to higher grounds. It was fortunate all the boys could swim although some were not strong swimmers.

Ake realized they were trapped but nevertheless, he composed himself not to alarm the innocent dozen. "This is just a high-low tide phenomenon. By tomorrow, the water will recede and we can leave the cave," he explained optimistically.

Low tide and high tide affect the rise and fall of sea levels. They are caused by the combined effects of the gravitational forces exerted by the moon and the sun and the rotation of the earth. It was getting darker. They retreated to the fork junction at Sam Yaek and found an elevated rocky ledge where they decided to camp overnight hoping the water would drop the next morning.

It was Night's birthday but no one care to celebrate it in a dark, damp cave surrounded by muddy floodwater.

Although they had camped in the open rugged hills before, this was the first time they had ever camped inside a cave. The stars were missing. The cave emitted a strange, earthy stench from the limestone. Although stale, it was still bearable. The boys made themselves as comfortable as possible like young boars in a pen.

⊷⊶

Water.

Water, water, water, everywhere.

That was the first thing Pong saw when he woke up. He did not sleep well. Neither did he know what time it was.

It was Saturday, June 24, 2018. Inside Tham Luang.

They thought they were safe. But, no. Muddy water was rushing in quickly with whirlpool-like circular movements. It looked like Hell had emptied her bowels of water and released its floodgates. The flood water was quickly filling up the cave. It hit the boys like a ton of bricks.

Ake was dead wrong. It was not a high-tide low-tide phenomenon. The water did not recede. He looked troubled.

"Move further in and look for higher ground!" Ake commanded as the boys retreated further back from Sam Yaek.

"It's raining cats and dogs," Tern hazarded an educated guess.

The heavens opened. The sky wept. It dawned upon them, it was the start of the monsoon season.

"The rainy season has begun unexpectedly earlier this year," regretted Ake, "Last year's rainy season began on July 15. It came three weeks earlier this year." However, none of them could hear the rain.

"Shucks!" Tee immediately cursed to himself, "Warangkana was spot on. A girl's intuition is deadly accurate. I'll be in the doghouse when I see her."

They realized they were in a bind – literally between the devil and the deep blue sea. The devil lay in the deep recess of the cavern and the muddy waters was the deep blue sea. Do they retreat deeper into the dark unknown recesses of the giant cavern or do they force their way out against the rising water?

It was a Hobson's choice. It was an illusion of two choices when there was only one – to go deeper in. The boys regretted discarding their slippers as they had to trek barefooted now. Not only were the paths slippery, sharp rocks protruded randomly. Some feet got cut and bruised.

"Arc we lost?" asked one Wild Boar.

"No, *ainoo*. We are not lost. We will make it out soon with the ropes," reassured Ake who continued to give hope to his defeated troop. Ake suggested that he dived to find out if he could go through the flood. If he did, then the boys would be safe.

"Adul, Night and Tee, hold on to the rope as I dived. If I pull the rope twice, it means you have to haul me back as I do not have enough oxygen. If I don't pull the rope, everyone can follow me," Ake instructed.

Shortly after, Ake pulled the rope twice. To say the least, the boys were disappointed.

The water was relentlessly invading the cave, conquering the space that was once empty. Ake now realized his mistake. "How I wish I could turn the clock back and check the weather forecast first!" he regretted. He realized he should take the 'Danger' sign-board at the entrance more seriously.

"*Ainoo*, we are stranded." Ake admitted his error apologetically. "It is raining heavily outside." Some thought there was an exit, so they retreated further into the cave.

Recede? The water did not. On the contrary, the twirling water was brutally unforgiving. The exit was well sealed by voluminous chocolate-colored water with strong underlying currents. Ake and the twelve boys heaved a huge, collective sigh of regret, blaming themselves.

Wild thoughts were jamming their brains. Whose decision was it to visit this cave? Shouldn't we have left a bit earlier before the rain rushed in? Was it a case of wrong place, wrong time? Did some-one utter something unpleasant to Jao Mae Nang Non? Would they blame the coach? Would there be a mutiny among the boys?

Wait. Did they seek permission from Jao Mae Nang Non before they entered the cave?

The muddy water was still advancing at breakneck speed with a strong tidal current. The potent force of the water reminded them of the Indonesian tsunami that hit Phuket in 2004.

Would the tsunami weaken?

CHAPTER SEVEN

Sunday, June 24, 2018.

Was June 24, 2018 the Apocalypse - the complete final destruction of the world? That was what certain quarters of Christian conspiracy theorists were inclined to believe. In the Book of Revelation, it is written: 'And there was given unto the beast a mouth speaking great things and blasphemies; and power was given unto him to continue forty-two months.' Combined with 666, the number of the beast, they deduced that June 24, 2018 marked the end of time.

The boys and their coach were marooned in the cave that was touted as a tourist attraction. How ironic!

It was complete darkness apart from the flashlight. It was worse than getting lost at night in the Thai jungle. At least, in the jungle, light was reflected from the distant stars unselfishly, even if the moon shied away. The Wild Boars had lost their sense of day and night although Ake's black military watch could tell. Their entire circadian rhythm was disrupted by the absence of daylight.

Every night before the boys hit the sack, Ake led them in prayers and sought blessings from Buddha, the enlightened one.

"Let me sleep well and not to worry about other things."

Tee enjoyed praying. He followed the teachings of Phra Khuva Boonchum Kruba, a famous forest meditation monk in northern Thailand, northeastern Myanmar and northern Laos.

⊶✦⊷

"Help me! Mummy!"

Suddenly, Mark, the second youngest, thought of mother and burst into a torrent of tears. His reptilian brain kicked into the survival mode instinctively, even as his intuitive brain forewarned him that danger was imminent.

The boys heard sound of water swooshed towards them. Shining their flashlights, they saw milky tea waters encircling to swallow them. It appeared as if an unseen giant hand was twirling the water. In less than an hour, the water rose by 10 feet.

It was a catch-22 dilemma. If they dived out against the water, they might be drowned. If they trudged further in, they might also die of hunger. They had made a decision quickly. Left with a difficult choice, the coach and the twelve kids escaped by hiking further in.

If the boys did not drink water in the first three days, their reptilian brains would switch to survival mode. The body stopped perspiration, urine and saliva production to conserve water. Toxins built up in the body as they were not flushed away by urine, resulting in aches and pains. As water content decreased, blood thickened and it forced the heart to pump harder and faster. A drop in blood pressure would cause coldness and sleepiness. There was a likelihood of heat fatigue and heatstroke as there was no perspiration.

The famished boys polished off whatever morsels of snacks they had bought for Night's birthday. Ake refused to eat any so that the boys could have more. Trained as a monk for a decade, Ake had a steel resolve to fast, and could overcome hunger without difficulty.

36

By now, all the water in their bottles had depleted. There was nary a drop in sharp contrast to the massive flood. After two days of being stranded, the boys started to feel tired.

"Don't drink from the muddy water as there is bacteria. It is unfit for drinking. It may contain sand, dirt and worse, excrement that could lead to typhoid, diarrhea or vomiting. It will cause severe dehydration," cautioned Ake, "I'll go further inside to look for water."

Ake switched on his flashlight and moved in. After a short while, he emerged and beckoned the boys to come nearer to him.

"*Ainoo*, it's safer to lick the moisture off the walls," Ake explained as the boys saw water dripping from the wall.

He demonstrated by licking the precious droplets of water like a starving dog. The rain, like other forces of nature, was a doubled-edged sword. While it blocked the exit, it seeped through the ground and dampened the walls. Now, they appreciated the proverb 'Every drop of water counts'. They continued to stay near the water source.

"Alternatively, you can lick the water remaining on stalagmites. It dripped from the stalactites above," Ake added, sharing his knowledge of cave survival.

Slowly but surely, the water was encroaching into their space. The twelve plus one shifted inside to higher ground for greater safety. Ake divided the boys into shifts.

"Let's take turns to dig the cave walls to get out," instructed Ake weakly in the hope of finding an exit. "At least, we are doing something. We do not want to wait around until the authorities find us." They boys searched for stones and used them to dig the walls. In between their tasks, they licked water off the wall. Over the next few days, they burrowed a tunnel fourteen feet into the cave.

As a leader, Ake crafted three management principles for survival. As repetition was the best form of communication, Ake recited them daily and assertively:

1. Be disciplined. Conserve energy. Use the flashlight only when necessary.

   Ake organized the twelve into shifts. In each shift, one boy would hold the flashlight daily to provide light. They had to conserve battery power in case they needed light for emergency purposes later. The batteries had a limited life span, especially when they were of a poorer grade. It was about being a minimalist, as Zen Buddhists practiced.

2. Create hope and willpower.

   Ake gave hope of a safe passage out of the cave for the boys. He fired the crucible and forged the iron will in them to survive. This meant banishing any negative thoughts, decluttering the mind, focusing on the "here and now" and practicing mindfulness.

3. Learn to understand nature.

   Ake taught them to appreciate the indomitable forces of nature. They could not go against them; only co-exist with them. It was about respecting nature and going with the flow. For safety, they must seek and remain on high ground. And only drink water from clean sources – like water dripping from the walls or on stalagmites. The porosity of limestone facilitated rainwater to seep through the ground and traveled to the cave. Most important, they must remember not to drink water from the flood.

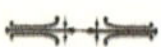

"Please count," Ake instructed periodically, adhering to safety instructions religiously.

"1, 2, 3, 4, 5, 6, 7, 8, 9, 10, 11 … 12."

"13." concluded Ake.

No one was missing.

Water was rushing in forcibly as if the doors of the department store opened for Black Friday. The force of water pushed some of the boys' legs, causing imbalance and tripping. If not for the rigorous football training to strengthen their calf muscles, more boys would have lost their balance. Gathering strength and leaning on others for support, they managed to inch themselves onto higher ground. There was nothing to cling on, only the unfriendly walls, that is, if they could. The lumps protruding out of the damp walls looked evil. And indeed, now the boys really felt abandoned, like stray dogs, in the rough part of the neighborhood.

The team clung onto the wall with all their might. They slipped. They wished they could spin a web and scale up the walls like their childhood hero, Spiderman. But no. There was no safety ledge they could walk on or handle they could grasp. By now, the light from the flashlight shone with less intensity.

The water became muddier. It looked precisely like the ubiquitous tea mixed with skimmed milk served in most roadside carts. The incessant rush of water left them with only one choice. The coach and his twelve charges were coerced to shift deeper inside. The higher ground was found on ledges on one side of the cave. They stood on the ledge trying to hold on to the wall for support. It was slippery smooth as if it was coated with engine oil. There was no traction at all. The minute they placed their bare hands on it, they slipped away easily.

Water again. Water, and more water everywhere. Like other elements of the earth, water could be a servant or a master. Water had many uses but in full force, it morphed into a Frankenstein that could devour the boys. The thirteen had crossed the Rubicon and there was no return.

"*Ainoo*, be brave. Stay firm on the ground. Hold on to the wall," Ake taught the boys to visualize imaginary bars on the wall and grip on them.

CHAPTER EIGHT

Hungry. Tired. Frightened.

After the first five nights with no food, the boys were extremely hungry and cried. They only had water dripping from the wall to lick. Luckily, the limestone was porous and rain water seeped through the ground above. It was cold comfort for them to know that with water, but without food, they could survive for thirty to forty days. At night, it was very cold and pitch-dark. They lay huddling together to generate warmth as their bodies gave out heat.

"We are thirsty and hungry," Mark, the second youngest of the team, murmured.

"I'm dizzy, weak and starving," said Titan. "I tried not to think of food, like fried rice or northern chili paste, because it'd make me even hungrier."

Call it a diversionary technique, resolute willpower or inner strength, it worked. While they tried to push away the idea of food, Mig, 13, started talking about congee, a Thai rice porridge, in his sleep.

When no food was consumed after a day, there would be intense hunger as energy from yesterday's food was used up. After two days, the hunger disappeared as the stomach shrunk. Without food but with water, cavers could survive for thirty to forty days. The body stored energy from fats and it supplied them to critical organs like the brain and heart. Without water, they could survive for more than a week only.

Despite being visibly weakened, Ake was convinced, as a captain, that he could not abandon a sinking ship. Although the boys and Ake were cut off from the world, they harbored a sliver of hope that rescuers would arrive soon.

This act of God was as close to the other world as Ake could get. The unforgiving water was still raging with all its might. Nevertheless, with every ounce of energy left in his body, Ake continued to give rays of hope to his team of young charges who had a promising future ahead of them. This is the basic essence of true servant leadership.

Unknown to them, the World Cup had produced some shocking results. South Korea scored two goals in injury time against Germany, while Belgium beat England 1-0.

⚊⟨⟩⚊

"Hurry up!"

"Follow me!" Ake screamed as the boys fearfully raced after him, imprinting footprints on the muddy ground.

It was pitch dark. The only source of light continued to be powered by cheap batteries. "The battery will be flat soon," Ake muttered. The light from the mobile phone was long gone.

They had already trudged four miles, their feet stomping heavily on muddy sediment and leaving behind deep impressions. Every time they moved forward, they needed to use force to lift each foot as it got stuck in the dense and sticky mud. It was a journey backwards to the unknown, dark side. No one knew when the water would stop, recede or whether it would continue to hunt them down. Why would it want to swallow up innocent, young boys?

With fear and anxiety written all over their faces, they were hiking deeper into the cave complex. The water was still chasing them and they had to move faster than the liquid. Oxygen levels dropped but it was sufficient to allow the boys to survive for a period.

The thirteen returned to the narrowest part of the cave which was barely five feet wide. Both the coach and the boys had to drag their bodies through in single file. Receiving minor cuts and abrasions from the sharp edges of the limestone rocks was expected. They spend a night camping at Pattaya Beach, far from the luxuries of the real Pattaya.

As the torrential water still flowed in angrily, they retreated. They trudged till they returned to Nern Nom Sao - now a small and dry mound higher than the flood waters. It measured 27 feet wide and 10 feet high, almost encircled by latte-colored water, 17 feet deep. The slopes were steep and rocky. On this elevated mound, they bundled themselves for warmth and security. It looked as if they were trapped in a runaway boat that had broken its chains from the mooring and drifted into the deep sea. This mound was probably half a mile from the top of the mountain, and two and a half miles from the entrance.

Mark surfaced his fears, "I wouldn't be able to go home,"

"Banish your negative thoughts. Be positive. Believe in the hope that we will emerge from the cave alive," Ake continued to motivate the boys, "never lose hope." Through mediation, Ake had a prescience a team of rescuers would appear.

"We always have hope!" Adul reaffirmed, "we continue to support each another."

When any of the boys was discouraged, Nick gave him moral support by shouting, "Hey! Fight! Fight! It will pass by you soon."

Conscious Meditation

Since the age of twelve, Ake studied Buddhism and practiced conscious meditation for ten years at the monastery. He could meditate up to an hour each time. Mediation is a key ritual in Buddhism. It is an ancient Asian practice where a person sits down and focuses their mind on a particular mantra or breathing pattern to achieve clarity, calmness and acceptance. Originating from Hinduism and Buddhism, it has been adopted widely by the corporate world, too.

Meditation reduces stress, anxiety and panic while increasing optimism, peace and wellbeing. Wandering thoughts in the mind are likened to monkeys jumping from tree to tree. Meditation tames the monkeys and silences the mind. It helps to lower the intensity of disturbances – flooding, in this case. It also improves empathy and promotes positivity, necessary for a team of isolated cavers staring at the jaws of imminent death.

With a decade worth of knowledge and experience, Ake taught the boys the techniques in "Conscious Meditation" to calm their anxiety, and conserve energy by limiting movements in confronting this life-or-death crisis. In a confined space with low levels of oxygen, slow and shallow breaths in sync with meditation prolonged their survival as they inhaled less oxygen. Regular meditation decluttered the mind of any negativity and focused on the present. The resulting calmness allowed them to figure out what to do next. Meditation kept the boys mentally strong.

Step by step, he gave clear instructions:

1. Sit down cross-legged with a straight back and rest both palms gently on the thighs.
2. Relax your body. Tell yourself you are stilling your mind and going to meditate for twenty minutes.
3. Close your eyes gently. Inhale and exhale slowly.
4. Be aware of your breathing while inhaling and exhaling.
5. Relax further.

6. Choose a beautiful object of consciousness, e.g. a flower, candle or feeling of peace and love.
7. Visualize your source of consciousness.
8. Allow your mind to dissolve and your body to disintegrate. Experience peace and love.
9. Still your mind. Experience no thoughts, feelings or images.
10. Continue to inhale and exhale gently and slowly.
11. Other thoughts may float in. Acknowledge them.
12. Accept your thoughts without judgment.
13. Return to focus on your breathing.
14. Inhale slowly… Hold your breath … Exhale slowly.
15. Towards the end of twenty minutes, tell yourself you will emerge in 10 seconds.
16. Count 13, 12, 11, 10, 9, 8, 7, 6, 5, 4, 3, 2 and 1.
17. Slowly open your eyes.
18. Be mindful of your current environment.

Later, Ake increased the duration of the meditation progressively to thirty, forty-five and finally, sixty minutes. Amongst the boys, Tee was the most proficient in meditation.

By the seventh day, besides losing physical energy and courage, they were also losing hope and patience. There was nothing else they could do. Claustrophobia was slowly but surely crawling into their minds. In a confined space over a long period, the boys could suffer from depression and anxiety. Adul fell to his knees in supplication,

"Lord, I'm only a boy. You're Almighty God. You're holy and You're powerful. Right now, I can't do anything. May You protect us. Come to help all thirteen of us. Thank You, God for everything that happened to my friends and myself. Amen."

The rest of the boys chorused, "Amen." Adul repeated the prayer and he felt more assured that the good Lord was protecting him.

Lost in the tunnel of time was Sunday, July 1. It was Note's 16th birthday Besides Night and Note, two other boys also spent their birthdays in the dark tunnels. There was little exuberance left to celebrate. Their survival took precedence over their birthdays.

In the dark days spent in the cave, Ake managed to keep track of the day and time with his trustworthy black SKMEI waterproof military watch. They were deprived of watching the World Cup matches. For the record, France had beaten Argentina 4-3, while Brazil beat Mexico 2-0.

It was getting colder and more humid. boys and their assistant coach were famished. Their days were numbered. Their skins were hugging their bones. They huddled together for warmth as their bodies generated heat. It protected the younger members. To conserve whatever ounce of energy remaining, they restricted their movement. It had an uncanny resemblance to a herd of twelve frightened and stressed wild boars headed by an alpha male, cornered against the wall by predators. They managed to sleep on and off for an hour or so.

Dom, reprising his role as captain of the team, urged the others as they lay side by side in total surrender.

"Fight on, don't despair!"

PART 2

Search and Rescue

DAY 1, JUNE 23 2018, SATURDAY

"Bad news."

"Boss, more than ten bicycles are parked outside the cave. Football boots and backpacks are strewn on the ground. I suspect some cavers are stuck inside. The entire entrance is flooded and the rain is still pouring," Anurak, a rugged Doi Nang Non forest park ranger, broke the news in cold sweat, without taking a breath. Dark clouds floated across the evening sky.

His boss, Nattapong, relayed the emergency to his immediate superior. This conversation sparked a chain of events that left the world teetering on the brink of a disaster for the next 17 days. The evacuation committee was hurriedly assembled and scrambled for immediate action.

Anurak, surveyed the black sky again. The heavy clouds continued to rain cats and dogs. Trees were swaying to and fro. Although bushes have a lower center of gravity, they were also punished by the bellowing winds. Small pebbles were blown off the paths and puddles of water were quickly ponding on the grass patches. The rate of water absorption by the ground was slower than the amount of rainfall. Such are the characteristics of a monsoon rain that are unseen in temperate countries.

Putting on his black raincoat, Anurak patrolled the cave entrance one more time to reconfirm what he had witnessed. This was his normal routine. Twice a day, once in the morning and once in the afternoon, he had to inspect the entrance, as dictated in his job specification.

He counted carefully this time. There were thirteen bicycles parked against the wooden railing. There were three racers and the rest were mountain bikes of different colors – blue, red and black and one white. Ten backpacks were scattered randomly on the ground. Some pairs of football shoes of assorted brands and shin guards were strewn around. Anurak checked the ghostly cave entrance again. It was deserted. There were no signs of human activity. Even if there was, it was drowned out by the incessant thunderous downpour which was like imprisoned water bursting a dam for freedom. His many years of patrolling experience intuited the cyclists had entered the cave. The entrance was swiftly flooding with more water. If ever anyone could emerge from the cave, he or she would have to swim and battle against the strong currents of monsoon rain.

The cave had its dangers - people have gone missing in Tham Luang before. And once monsoon season starts in July and ends in October, the cave transforms from an innocuous sanctuary to a lethal trap – from an angel to a monster. The water can flood up to 16 feet. It is only safe to visit the cave between November and April.

Were there thirteen cave explorers? Who were they? Were they tourists or Thais? Were they adults or students?

⚊⊰⊱⚊

20 missed calls.

After coaching the senior footballers in a match, Nopparat Khanthavong, checked his phone. He had been the head coach of

Wild Boars Football Academy for several years. Twenty missed calls were from parents of his junior team. He swung into panic mode.

He rang Ake immediately. There was no answer. Fear was written all over his face. He rang a number of boys in quick succession. The lines were dead. He froze.

Finally, Nopparat was able to reach Songpol, 13. His mother had picked him up after training. So, Songpol was the only one who did not visit the cave.

"They have gone exploring in Tham Luang," Songpol let the cat out of the bag.

Nopparat's heart sank immediately.

He raced frantically to the cave only to find bicycles, backpacks and shoes abandoned by the railing. Water engulfed its entrance.

"Ake! Ake! Ake!" he shouted.

His body went numb and cold.

⚊⊰ ⊱⚊

"It's already eight!"

The clock chimed eight times.

"What time did Night say he'll be back?"

"On the dot at seven," clarified Phunphatsa, Night's sister. She made several calls to both Nopparat and Ake. They went unanswered.

"Maybe he's late. It's raining heavily," suggested Night's mum, comforting herself.

Phunphatsa rang Nick's mother, "Is Nick back from football training?"

"No, I'm still waiting for him."

Several boxes of assorted sizes, wrapped in colorful paper, were arranged neatly on a square table at the side of the living room.

On this day, Saturday, June 23, 2018, Night turned 17 - a significant milestone that young men wanted to mark and celebrate in style. When the key is received this day, boys turn to men. It is a rite of passage where young men would experience the newfound freedom in adulthood.

A bright yellow SpongeBob SquarePants birthday cake was idling in the refrigerator waiting for Night to cut it.

Seventeen candles stood ready to be planted into the cake. Phunphatsa prepared an additional one for good luck. It represented 'one for good measure'. They were waiting for Night to blow out the candles and make a wish.

Slightly after eight, Night's family and relatives were still waiting patiently. There was no sight of Night. Neither was there any sound from him. The mood was somber. As the minute hand ticked, anxiety grew in tandem.

Night's mother quietly made her way to the altar facing the main door. Looking pensively at Buddha, positioned one foot above her eyes, she whispered a silent prayer with her head bowed with two clasped hands. The face of Buddha was so serene that he lent an aura of calmness instantly. He was a symbol of hope, tranquility and spirituality that influenced his worshippers to overcome anger, greed, and hatred. A practicing Buddhist, she viewed life with a different pair of lenses, living a daily life of compassion, detachment and impermanence.

Would her faith move mountains?

***

"*Pee* Tee, Are you back home?"

No response.

Warangkana, Tee's girlfriend, was texting with both her thumbs continuously. Visibly upset at the lack of response, she was clueless on the next move. A boy's silence is a girl's greatest fear. Silence on the other hand could spell imminent danger. All negative images of the worst possible scenarios flashed across her mind. Did he find someone new? Did my shouting upset him? What can I do to recover my fault?

"*Pee* Tee, do you have to be like this when you go to Tham Luang?"

She was attempting a sympathetic angle to draw a response from Tee.

Warangkana continued firing a barrage of texts, unconsciously exerting more pressure on the phone's keyboard.

No response.

Her intuition nudged her that something was wrong. Was he lost inside the cave where there was no signal? A girl's intuition is usually right. In a final desperate attempt, like a drowning girl clutching at a straw, she shot an SOS text to the coach, Nopparat and his assistant, Ake:

"Where have you guys been? Dom isn't online either."
"Nobody's online."
The silence was deadly.

⇥⇤

"My son, come on out! I am waiting for you here!"

"When are you coming home, my boy? I'm here to pick you up!"

"Please hurry up and come home! My son, let's go home together!"

Anguished parents cried and shouted for their kids at the cave entrance. They pleaded aloud to the spirit of the cave, Jao Mae Nang Non, to accede to their desperate prayers to release their trapped sons.

"My boy, come home!" wailed Kamaei Promthep, grandmother of Dom. She knew he was in danger.

Earlier, Dom's aunt asked his friends in a group chat where were the boys. Out came the dreadful answer she did not want to hear: the boys had gone to the cave.

⇥⇤

Ring! Ring! Ring!

Earlier at 9 pm, Sungwut Kummongkol answered the phone.

"The boys went for football practice at the fields and proceeded to visit the cave," cried the mother of one young boy.

It was raining heavily. Sheets of water were pounding the grounds of Tham Luang-Khun Nam Nang Non Forest Park forcefully.

By 10 pm, Sungwut had gathered a team of 14 rescue workers from Nam Nang Non Forest Park and Mae Sai Rescue Team and led them to Tham Luang. They were among the first teams to race to the cave. After they set up lighting, they were stunned to see the boy's bicycles parked at the cave entrance. Football boots, shin pads and backpacks were strewn around. A blue jacket and a green plastic bag hung over the first bicycle's handlebars.

Sungwut had a bad hunch – the boys were trapped inside and their exit was sealed off by the flood.

The rescuers entered the first part of the cave but the small hole leading further in was flooded. To get through it, they had to dive. As they lacked diving equipment, they retreated. Sungwut contacted the Sirikorn Chiang Rai Rescue Team for reinforcements.

DAY 2, JUNE 24, SUNDAY

"I arrive at the cave around 1 am. At first, I thought it was a normal case of lost children; just that there were more children involved," recalled Narongsak Osottanakorn, Governor of Chiang Rai, who was informed of the missing boys. Quickly, he assumed the Commander of Rescue Mission. He graduated from Ohio State University with a Master degree in geodetic engineering and geology.

Sirikorn Chiang Rai Rescue Team with 22 divers and rescuers arrived with their diving equipment. Soldiers and local administration officers pitched in with the rescue. Alas, they failed to dive through because their oxygen tanks were stuck during the dive. After assessing the situation carefully, they concluded that diving through the flood was impossible. They pulled out as the rain was pounding and the water level was rising. They believed the boys had retreated deeper into the cave - beyond the flooded area which they could not access. No one knows the extent of the flooding inside the cave although they could assess the situation at the entrance.

"How are you going to get the boys out quickly?" the mother cried out again, as other families joined her to keep vigil outside Tham Luang.

It put a lot of pressure on the rescuers. The silhouettes of the bicycles sent shivers down their spines even as it triggered the tears of the parents.

"I hope they are safe. I still have hope. I hope that all thirteen will come out safely," prayed Sungwu. After a discussion, they concluded they could not continue the search on their own. The rescue operation needed expert help.

At 2 am, the phone rang to break the silence of the unearthly hour. Vernon Unsworth's deep sleep was disturbed and he woke up dreamily. He was better known as Vern.

"The children are missing at Tham Luang. Can you come and help?" came the distress call.

Originally from England, Vern, 63, lived near Tham Luang now. His wife, in her 40s, was the Vice President of Tambon Huai Khrai in Mae Sai. He had over 40 years of caving experience. For the last six years, he had explored and dived in Tham Luang extensively. He knew the spooky cave so intimately that it had become his second home. Vern was probably the best caver to navigate the interiors of the snaking cave.

Ruengrit Changkwanyuen, 42, was among the first volunteer cave divers to arrive with his equipment. The vicious current tore off his mask when he did not fasten it securely. An information technology launch manager in General Motors Thailand, he had spent years exploring shipwrecks in Michigan's Great Lakes and cave diving in Florida.

"It was like walking into a strong waterfall and feeling the water rushing at you," he said. "It was a horizontal climb against the water with every move."

The search was halted before dawn. In the morning, the Tourist Police's silver pick-up truck transporting Vern came to a screeching halt at the cave.

"I was actually scheduled to go into the cave on June 24 anyway," Vern explained, "I got all my gear ready, and I was going in to do a solo trip just to see what the water levels were like."

No one could have predicted the flood which came uninvited, three weeks earlier than in the previous years. Last year, the flood arrived only on July 15.

"These kids were just totally unlucky. Wrong place, wrong time," Vern surmised, "It happened very quickly. You can't blame the coach, you can't blame the kids."

The local rescue team co-led by Vern began their search. Footprints and handprints of the boys were found. After an exploratory assessment, he concluded this crisis necessitated international expertise and specialized equipment. He wrote to the Thai authorities:

Time is running out!

1. **ROB HARPER**
2. **RICK STANTION MBE**
3. **JOHN VOLANTHEN**

They're the world best cave divers.
Please contact them through

UK EMBASSY ASAP

He urged them to alert cave rescue associations in the United Kingdom for immediate assistance. They had invaluable experience in similar rescue missions in the past. Vern himself had assisted in cave rescue operations in United Kingdom before but they were "nothing on this scale."

Narongsak declared the Tham Luang–Khun Nam Nang Non Forest Park a disaster zone. The Tham Luan Rescue Operation Center was quickly established. Tham Luang was Ground Zero. A request was urgently escalated to the Thai Navy SEALs Team headquarters for their immediate assistance. His Majesty, The King of Thailand provided meals for the rescue officers and journalists. Three military trucks were hurriedly converted into kitchens. In each kitchen were five volunteer officers whipping up meals to be packed into food boxes for one to five thousand diners daily. Hordes of volunteers worked day and night to provide various services for the rescuers. The King also donated basic necessities – LED lightbulbs, diving suits, mosquito repellent, raincoats, hats, overalls with socks and boots.

Volunteers transported rescue equipment into the cave

Volunteers from Jitarsa (the spirit of volunteering in Thai) Project helped to clean up Tham Luang. This project was initiated royally for Thais to engage in community activities for the common good nationwide. Its tagline read 'We Do Good From the Heart'.

What was meant to be a leisurely daytrip for Vern was extended unceremoniously into a 17-day nail-biting rescue operation.

A sheet of paper was passed around for the world's best divers with their contact details, and Bangkok was able to bring them to Tham Luang within 24 hours.

DAY 3, JUNE 25, MONDAY

At 2.45 am, a team of 20 Thai Navy SEALs led by Captain Anan Surawan, Commander of the First Special Warfare Corps, arrived with diving equipment. They alternated the search with the volunteer rescue teams. Both proceeded slowly and cautiously into the winding tunnels of the eerie cave, giving their personal safety the top priority.

It took an hour for the Thai Navy SEALs to reach Chamber Three which the rescuers could not reach. One section was under seven feet of water. Vern informed them there was a small hole which they could dive through. When they would emerge, there was a small sand bank on the right. The boys were most likely to be stranded there.

The Thai Navy SEALs managed to dive through the hole. New footprints and handprints were discovered but there was no sign of the boys. Meanwhile, in the surroundings, volunteers found a new passage but it did not connect to Tham Luang.

Accustomed to clear and calm seas, the Thai Navy SEALs were strangers to cold muddy waters and strong currents. With zero

A Thai Navy SEAL dived to survey the flooded cave

experience in cave diving, their diving equipment was ill-suited for cave rescue. In cases of emergencies in open seas, they could surface for air - an impossible act for some parts of the cave which were fully flooded.

As the rain continued pounding, the Thai Navy SEALs fought a losing battle against, surprisingly, nature – a torrential and fast-rising flood.

"When the Thai Navy SEALs went into the cave, they couldn't see anything because the water was so muddy. So, they came back," explained Chaiyon Srisamut, a friend of Vern.

The boys were hemmed in by the rising flood. The rescuers believed the boys retreated to Pattaya Beach, an elevated ground with an air pocket. Without making any headway, the rescue teams regrouped the next morning.

The Provincial Electricity Authority from Chieng Mai installed cables and supplied electricity for the lights. One of its staff, Praksong, toiled non-stop for the first three days, sleeping only

3 to 4 hours per day. The flooding and tight working space were the main challenges. Praksong's greatest fear was snakes lurking in the dark. He prayed for the boys' safety although he thought some of them would not survive the calamity.

DAY 4, JUNE 26, TUESDAY.

"**M**om is here to receive you," wailed one woman hysterically. Makeshift shrines were hastily set up for traditional rituals. Local Thais offered prayers, incense and food while shamans sacrificed live animals to appease the spirit, Jao Mae Nang Non. The boys' families had been camping in the mud, praying outside the entrance to the cave, close to where the boys had left their bicycles.

"We still have hope," cried Phunphatsa, Night's sister,

The persistent rains complicated the rescue effort. The divers re-entered the cave and discovered the water had almost reached the ceiling. They needed to surface for air. Besides that, they needed a dry area to check their equipment and the oxygen level in their tanks. The water had to be pumped out.

More workers from the government department and other volunteers arrived with equipment to generate electricity and to pump water out over 2 miles. They labored within a dimly lit confined space and a tight deadline. The second attachment of Navy SEALs arrived to augment the first team. A total of 127 Navy

Villagers praying to The Reclining Goddess

SEALs, current and former, assisted in the operation. A team of Border Patrol Police and forest soldiers was also summoned to lend a hand.

Vern and a Navy SEALs team continued their search with the deployment of a remote-controlled submarine in the flood. Two thermal camera-installed drones flew over the forest to look for any cavity that might lead to the cave.

Volunteers preparing hose to pump out water

The rain generated thick and sticky mud within the cave. The mud stuck onto the boots of the rescuers and sucked them down making progress arduous. The divers reached the fork junction at Sam Yaek. However, they were forced back by the rushing flood that clogged a choke point – a narrow tunnel - near Pattaya Beach. One volunteer diver shouted, "Never give up!"

Laos deployed an award-winning rescue team, "Vientiane 1623", to assist in the rescue. In 2016, this team won the prestigious Magsaysay Award, the Asian equivalent of the Nobel Prize.

Princess Ubolratana Rajakanya, the eldest child of King Bhumibol Adulyadej and Queen Sirikit, drew a picture of a smiling wild boar with the twelve boys and their coach perching on its back. At the bottom of the drawing was #Welcome Home with a heart sign.

Prime Minister, Prayut Chan-o-cha rallied Thailand to lend a hand and support the rescue efforts.

RRRRING!

5944 miles away, in the rolling hills of Derbyshire in England, summer had barely started a week ago. The hot sunshine at 80 degrees Fahrenheit contrasted greatly with the earlier harsh, wet winter. Bill Whitehouse was at home, whipping up a lunch of eggs and bacon. He was the vice chairman of the British Cave Rescue Council (BCRC) and a retired cave diver.

Formed in 1967, BCRC is a coordinating, not a governing, body. Its members comprise of 15 volunteer cave rescue organizations which are entirely autonomous. It facilitates the exchange of information between them and provides a common platform for them.

The phone rang. Bill was summoned to fly to Bangkok immediately. BCRC raised its alarm and activated three members - John Volanthen, an IT consultant; Rick Stanton, a former firefighter; and Robert Harper, a cave diving veteran.

Bill dropped everything and started to pack his equipment. His wife finished cooking his lunch and looked after their grandchildren.

On the next Thai Airways flight to Bangkok, three seats were reserved by the Royal Thai Embassy in South Kensington, London. John, Rick and Robert hurriedly made their way to Heathrow Airport in London.

The cave diving community is close-knit. The number of divers in the world who are able to extract lost cavers in flooded caves can be counted within ten fingers.

<u>John Volanthen</u>
John, 47, an Englishman, worked as an IT consultant in Bristol, UK. He began cave diving through a social club when he attended De Montfort University. He was a volunteer cave diver who specialized in cave rescues with Rick Stanton.

In 2010, he was in a team with Rick that staged an unsuccessful cave rescue of Eric Establie in the Dragonnière Gaud Cave,

France. He assisted in the recovery of the body of Polish cave diver Artur Kozłowski from a cave in Kiltartan, Ireland in 2011. A couple of years later in 2014, he assisted in the recovery of the bodies of two Finnish divers from Jordbrugrotta cave in Norway. After diving down to the cave, he and his colleagues decided not to proceed as the operation was too complex.

John designed and constructed some of his own diving equipment - compacting rebreathers and making them more efficient. He also designed a mapping device that collected information as he dived.

Richard Stanton

Richard, 57, was a firefighter in England for 25 years before retirement. Also known as Rick, he attended Aston University, where he joined both the caving and diving clubs.

In 2004, he was in a team that rescued six British cavers who were trapped in the Alpazat caverns in Mexico for eight days due to a flash flood.

Rick developed two closed-circuit rebreather units. It created cave diving depth records. He modified the rebreather to be worn on the sides of the body rather than the chest or back. This facilitated swimming through narrower passageways. He prototyped his designs and tested them in swimming pools before using them in caves.

He also used underwater scooters to dive more efficiently, traveling greater distances while conserving energy and oxygen supplies.

Robert Harper

Robert, 70, was a veteran potholing expert from Somerset.

Bill Whitehouse, vice chairman of the British Cave Rescue Council described John and Rick as the "A Team". They had established a reputation as being among the greatest cave rescue divers on the planet. Both were volunteers with the South and Mid Wales

Cave Rescue Team. In 2010, John, Rick and two others, Jason Mallinson and René Houben, set a world record for the longest cave penetration dive, 5.5 miles, into the Pozo Azul cave in Spain.

Bill praised, "They have been at the spearhead of making their way through because they have the skills and expertise to do it."

DAY 5, JUNE 27, WEDNESDAY

After a long flight of eleven hours, aided by tail winds, the trio landed at Bangkok and transferred to an internal flight of an hour and fifteen minutes north to Chiang Rai. The three selfless Brits, arguably the world's most elite cave divers, were the first foreign team to arrive. Looking like any other ordinary rescuer, they did not attract any attention. Supervised by Robert Harper, they conducted reconnaissance dives with their custom-built diving equipment. They were confronted with a mammoth assignment, fraught with dangers and unknowns.

"It was a race against time," Vern recalled, "They needed world-class divers and that's what we got. They went straight into the cave. That's when things really started to happen." Vern hand sketched the map of the cave for John and Rick which they memorized.

"At that stage, there was no way they could get anywhere near the boys. Conditions were really quite bad, the water flow was very strong and the suspended sediment made visibility very low. To be honest, the chances of getting far were not high," Bill admitted.

John Volanthen did his first exploratory dive

When the divers dived into the cave, they had to battle against the raging torrent. When they dived out, they were swimming with the current. However, the first diver would stir up the silt, causing cloudiness for the second diver, which would intensify for the third. Visibility was extremely poor.

Half of the equipment transported to Chamber Three malfunctioned as they were damaged by knocks against the wall. The command center admitted it was the first time they encountered such a challenge. They did not have the right expertise or equipment. So, they started to source for the right equipment.

One search team found a passageway. However, it led to a dead end. The unforgiving rain continued to fall treacherously. Flood waters reached a critical level.

Her Royal Princess Chulabhorn, the youngest daughter of King Bhumibol Adulyadej and Queen Sirikit, gave her moral encouragement to the rescuers. She personally donated $15,000 to support the search and rescue operations.

A team of 17 United States Air Force para-rescuemen and survival specialists, along with 13 support staff based on the Japanese island of Okinawa landed at 1 am and rushed to the cave directly. Maroon-beret para-rescuemen were generally tasked with recovery and medical treatment of personnel in humanitarian and combat environments. Their motto: "These Things We Do, That Others May Live".

US embassy spokesperson, Jillian Bonnardeaux, from the US Indo-Pacific Command (USPACOM) said, "Our Operators are trained in personnel recovery tactics and techniques and procedures." They all brought along high-technology equipment, including 3D infra-red scanners and satellite-linked geological survey monitors.

Jessica Tait, 30, an Air Force captain and public affairs officer, felt a strong hope among the international teams. She was born in Seoul to a Korean mother and American father who served in the US Air Force in South Korea.

"One thing I'd like to note about the mood in this camp is that we've all been in here as a family, working together, and I never sensed anyone being demotivated," she said.

DAY 6, JUNE 28, THURSDAY

The search continued despite the incessant monsoon rain and rising flood levels. While setting up the pumps, the divers could not dive. The pump discharging the water failed to keep in tandem with the torrential downpour. Mother Nature overwhelmed the man-made machinery.

Meanwhile, outside the cave, rescue teams were strategically sub-divided into smaller nimble-footed groups to scour for alternative passages into the cave. More information was requested from local villagers. Hiking over 13 miles, it bore immediate results.

Led by Vern, a team of a hundred men from the Department of National Parks, Wildlife and Plant Conservation, including soldiers and policemen, spotted a 70-foot shaft at Doi Pha Mee. As the shaft was tight, a small-built and experienced National Park Rescue member, Wutthiphong Mueansutthiwong was lowered. There was little air and the rocks were hard to dig through. There was also a danger that huge rocks could fall on him. He descended 120 feet further. Disappointingly, it led to a dead-end.

Pumping out flood water

Another team, led by the national police chief, Pol. Gen. Chakthip Chaichinda, continued their search to the north of this shaft.

Narongsak related, "A border policeman managed to get into the cave through the shaft which is about 130 feet deep. The cave floor was muddy but it led to nowhere."

Appropriately called "boxes of hope" were the Rubbermaid-like rectangular plastic boxes containing a bottle of water, a packet of Kleenex wipes, a milk-flavored croissant, bread and biscuits. These were dropped into cavities in the mountain in the hope they would reach the trapped boys. They were also floated on underground rivers. A message from the National Police Chief read: 'If received, then reply and show on the map where you are. Everybody will quickly help.' A map was also enclosed in these airtight and leak-proof boxes with four interlocking clips each. If the boys received these "boxes of hope", they could indicate their location to the rescuers. Every idea was explored. Nothing was left to chance.

Sutthisak Sornlum, chief of the Soil Engineering Development and Research Center in Kasetsart University, suggested the possibility of drilling the shaft. It was about 1,700 feet above the cave entrance and the same distance from Pattaya Beach. To drill the shaft, a helicopter must lift a drilling machine to the top of the mountain. It would be both dangerous and time-consuming. If a new shaft was found, they would have to drill through the walls to reach Pattaya. As of today, no technology is capable of detecting cavers trapped deep underground.

The American team joined in the search. By eight in the evening, the continuous downpour and the rising tide had blocked the entire entrance of the cave. The noise from the rain and currents was deafening and the whole atmosphere looked hostile. The search came to a sudden halt. Pumping had also stopped as the rainfall was overwhelming. Everyone was discouraged. The command center announced they would rethink their strategy for the search.

Meanwhile, the water draining team searched for the source of the spring that flowed into the cave. They intended to block it and divert the water away from Tham Luang.

At Tham Luang's entrance, someone scribbled the mission of the rescue on a white board:

WE'RE HERE 4 THE SAME PURPOSE
JOINT TASK FORCE OPERATION ETHICS

- RESPECT!!!
- SPEAK HUMAN LANGUAGE
- COMMUNICATE: Clear, concise and direct to the point.
- RESPECT DIVERSITY
- NO DISCRIMINATION
- NO IDEA IS STUPID IDEA

We're only one TEAM

DAY 7, JUNE 29, FRIDAY

The water expert team arrived from Japan International Co-operation Agency (JICA) to expedite the water draining. They succeeded in reducing the flood level. Their two Kubota pump trucks installed with high-pressure water pumps donated for the Ayutthaya irrigation project were summoned to Tham Luang to accelerate the draining efforts. The Japanese also provided radar topographical maps created with satellite data at maximum resolution from the Advanced Land Observing Satellite 2.

The torrential rain unleashed its anger again. Prime Minister Prayut Chan-o-char visited the site to comfort the families of the missing boys. He also inspired the team to keep their hopes high. After leading a meditation session, he encouraged the volunteers by helping in the cooking.

Officials comforted the frantic families by repeating that some of the boys knew the cave well, having visited it a few times. Moreover, the boys were tough. They could survive the entrapment by drinking rainwater.

In the evening, a team of diving experts from Beijing Peaceland Foundation arrived. The six-man rescue team brought rescue

*The Monk of Three Nations came out of solitary meditation
to pray for the lost boys*

equipment including underwater robots, diving equipment and a three-dimensional spectrometer. Underwater robots could gather and send information back on the water depth and condition of the cave. The team had experience in life-saving rescues in Myanmar and Nepal.

Phra Khuva Boonchum, 54, visited the cave. In Myanmar, he was known as Maing Hpone Sayadaw. Since the age of thirteen, this forest meditation monk had a huge following in Thailand, Myanmar and Laos. Hence, he was revered as 'The Monk of Three Nations'. This lifelong vegetarian was noted for his long and solitary periods of meditation in caves. Observing silence, he survived on fruits and biscuits left by devotees outside his cave. He always walked barefoot everywhere he went.

Believed to possess psychic powers, he performed religious rites and prayed for the thirteen as well as for the spirit that ruled Tham Luang - Jao Mae Nang Non. Some believed he was the reincarnation of her stable boy lover.

He comforted the boys' families and encouraged the rescuers by blessing the Khuva Boonchum Holy Thread worn on their wrists. On his departure, he predicted,

"They are all still there; they will be found in one or two days."

DAY 8, JUNE 30, SATURDAY

Incredulous as it might seem, the rain that was pouring relentlessly for days obeyed the monk's prayers. It suddenly stopped and remained so until the boys were found on Monday, July 2. Many Thais believe the monk interceded to halt the rain. When the rain ceased, it was easier to pump the water out. The monstrous flood had single-handedly forced the divers to be routed.

A second Chinese team from the Green Boat Emergency Rescue organization arrived. "Our skills are search and rescue on mountains and in caves. We hope we can help," said Wang Xudong, a member of the group.

Up to 20 Australians arrived including six police divers, one navy diver and 100 pounds of diving equipment. "The complexity and scale of the cave was unknown," expressed commander Glen McEwen from the Australian federal police.

Among the 20 Australians was Dr. Richard Harris, 53. British divers specifically identified Dr. Harris as the linchpin in the rescue operation. In fact, the 'highest levels' in the Thai government had summoned him to help. Dr. Harris worked as the Head of Unit of South Australia Ambulance Service (SAAS) MedSTAR Emergency

Medical Retrieval. This organization's website described him as someone who combines a 'taste for adventure with his medical practice' and as having 'a lifelong interest in the underwater world'.

Dr. Harris had experienced cave diving explorations in Australia, China, Christmas Island and New Zealand. An anesthetist by training, he specialized in expedition medicine and retrieval operations. He was also known for his work in medical assistance during natural disasters in the Pacific region, including Australia and Vanuatu. As soon as the call arrived, the Adelaidean diver immediately suspended his holiday in Thailand and stepped forward.

Dr. Andrew Pearce, MedSTAR Director of Clinical Services said of him, "Harris' medical knowledge and technical expertise have made him a go-to person for these types of operations."

"He has just got so much experience of diving in so many different places around the world," praised Michael Eaton, another of Dr. Harris' friends.

Dr Harris' dive partner is Craig Challen. They were diving mates in a closely knitted group called the Wet Mules. It originated from a rare American saying that a wealthy man had 'enough money to burn a wet mule'. It occurred to them they were likened to wet mules diving in cold waters and transporting heavy objects in and out of caves. So, they adopted the name of 'Wet Mules' appropriately. Known as the 'Formula One of diving', they were well respected for their skill, experience and courage in cave diving.

Craig, a veterinary surgeon in Perth, was getting ready for his holiday when the phone rang. He quickly reconfigured his holiday luggage and made it to the airport in 45 minutes. In 2010, he made a record-setting 640-foot dive whilst caving in New Zealand. He was Dr. Harris' diving partner.

Water levels dropped and visibility improved. Together with the Thai Navy SEALs and two Australians, the British trio dived deeper into the bowels of the cave. They used their fingers and thumbs to ensure they had a route mapped out.

"One of the first things they had to do in pushing through was to lay a guide line so that they could get out again and so others could follow along," Bill explained. "Underwater, it's completely dark. You have lots of light on your head but there's a lot of mud and suspended sediment. You can't see much. It's like driving in fog with your headlights on."

After driving over 600 miles, Panom Cheanpirom arrived in the morning with three giant water pumps, since the government pumps were too small.

"I felt bad for the kids, wondering how they would survive and what they would eat as it was dark in the cave," Panom said, watching the parents sitting and waiting at the cave entrance. His compassion for the boys led him to help in any way he could.

The three gigantic pumps were installed at Tham Sai Thong, next to Tham Luang. It bore results gradually. The water receded. Over 800 square miles of rice paddy fields were flooded.

A geologist, Chaiporn Siripornpibul, was summoned to analyze the flow pattern of the water. He discovered the water in Tham Luang was higher and flowed into the connecting Tham Sai Tong cave, east of the mountain.

Outside, various overland teams continued to search for shafts and scanned the thickness of the walls around the air pocket in Pattaya Beach. Meanwhile, a short distance away, the medical teams rehearsed evacuation procedures by both road ambulances and helicopters. At least six white ambulances, serially numbered, and two white Royal Thai Police helicopters were spotted.

After a long flight from Germany where she had attended a search-and-rescue (SAR) dog training program, Jing Jing heard Tham Luang needed SAR dogs to verify scent emitting from cavities in the mountain. A volunteer with the Thailand Rescue Dog Association, she took a 15-hour overland trip together with Seeker,

A *search-and-rescue dog sniffed for the lost boys*

a German Shepherd and the only certified volunteer SAR dog in the rescue. Seeker was first brought to the cave to smell clothing belonging to the missing children. Together, Jing Jing and Seeker searched for holes in the mountain and verified the scents. Some of the holes were 80 degrees steep, muddy and lined with sharp rocks. Two other police dogs were also helping to sniff out the lost boys. Forty rescuers from the Department of Disaster Prevention and Mitigation also arrived to intensify the rescue.

DAY 9, JULY 1, SUNDAY

"Where do you think the boys are likely to be?"

"This is probably around about the best place they could be," Vern replied, pointing to Pattaya Beach.

Thai police interviewed the villagers to extract more clues. The Thai Navy SEALs identified a team member of the Wild Boars who had skipped the cave expedition. He vaguely recalled that he and his other team mates had visited a spot in the cave before – and it sounded like Pattaya Beach.

The prayers of Phra Khuva Boonchum were answered. The flood level receded and the search resumed.

Trudging through milky-tea floodwater, wriggling through slippery crevices and trekking on muddy paths, the divers reached a large cavern just before the fork junction at Sam Yaek. The flood level was low enough for rescuers to walk through. Coupled with the fact that it was prominent, spacious and safe, the commanders secured it as a key base where the Thai Navy SEALs would be stationed. Thai Navy SEAL Captain Anan Surawan was appointed as the Head of Forward Operating Base which was called Chamber

Three. Divers would use it as their starting point to dive. Hundreds of oxygen tanks were transported here so that divers could stay in the cave longer.

"Everyone was aware it was dangerous. But my men did not hesitate to dive. I saw it in their eyes that they were ready to sacrifice," commented Thai Navy SEAL commander, Rear Admiral Apakorn Yuukong-kaew with pride.

The Thai Navy SEALs soldiered on and reached the fork junction at Sam Yaek. They were rewarded with evidence of footprints. It gave them hope that the thirteen were not too far away. The rescue commander, Narongsak, believed the boys were one to two miles away. Apart from this, however, there were no other signs that the boys were alive.

Slippers and bags belonging to the boys were found

John and Rick arrived at the flooded Pattaya Beach which is usually dry from December to June. Their plan was to dive and reach the kids as soon as possible. To wait for Thai Navy SEALs to lay guide ropes section by section would be too slow, so they agreed to lay the ropes themselves. Each diver took four tanks with him. The journey to and fro approximated five hours. A huge support team monitored their dives from Chamber Three. Nothing was heard from the duo for the next 23 hours.

Concurrently, for four consecutive days, both expert and volunteer overland teams continued to comb every square foot of Doi Nang Non mountain. They searched for alternative shafts to the cave but failed to find any. The only way to rescue the boys was through the cave. The divers redoubled their efforts with the underwater hunt.

Her Royal Highness Princess Soamsawali, former wife of King of Thailand, presided over the National Scouts Day. She spoke to Deputy Prime Minister, Air Chief Marshall Prachin Chantong, "I've followed the news about the missing boys in Chiang Rai. Haven't they found them? Please give my moral support to them and the rescue operation officers. I've learned that it's very difficult. I hope the boys are found soon. I'm worried about them."

DAY 10, JULY 2, MONDAY

After clearing the first section, the next 500 meters was very challenging. Stalactites blocked the narrow passageway. The water was freezing. John and Rick were cold.

Gradually, the British duo reached Pattaya Beach which was flooded. A Wild Boars team member who had visited the cave previously but declined joining the team this time, believed the boys were stranded here. There was no sight nor sign of any life. So, John and Rick pushed themselves deeper through to install thick guide ropes of 0.4 inch thick. Using the guide rope, they swam in the right direction as well as pulled themselves against the currents.

At around 10 pm, when the rope ran out, John surfaced up from the waters in a narrow rocky outcrop – Nern Non Sao, a quarter mile from Pattaya Beach.

"Wherever there is air space, we surface, we shout, we smell," explained John, "It's a standard procedure for such rescue operations. We smelt the children before we saw or heard them." One of the smell cave rescue divers recognized was human excrement.

John headlights pointed towards the elevated rocky mound. Miraculously, they were rewarded with an 'eureka' moment. It startled the skin-and-bones boys who were nestled closely together. Like frightened fawns caught in the headlights of a jeep in the jungle at night, they emerged disoriented behind a rock and made their way down the rocky ledge three feet above the flood water which was lapping against the rocks. The boys were pleasantly shocked at the arrival of the twin saviors suited in black.

Rick witnessed the momentous minute the boys emerge from behind a rock to the muddy ledge. He recounted, "That was a massive, massive relief. Initially we weren't certain they were all alive - as they were coming down the slope, I was counting them until I got to 13. Unbelievable. We couldn't see them initially - they had to come round the corner." Rick could not believe what his eyes saw, and exclaimed, "They're all alive!"

Had John's guide line been five yards shorter, he would, most likely, have missed the air pocket. Call it a stroke of luck, predestination or divine intervention.

Earlier, the boys were digging the walls with stone fragments at top of the rocks when they heard voices. They were unsure if they were human voices. They stopped and listened but did not believe someone was there. It turned out the voices were from men and they were shocked. Mig, who had a torch, approached them. The boys were surprised, he was not a Thai.

John called out, "Raise your hands."

Adul cried, "Thank you." It was divine intervention that there were two boys -Adul and Bew - who could speak English was in this lost team.

John asked cautiously, "How many of you?"

Adul, struggling for the right word, replied, "Thirteen." His brain was functioning at slow speed after nine days of entrapment. He thought a lot before he came up with an answer in English.

John: "Thirteen?"

Adul: "Yeah, yeah."

Diver: "Brilliant."

Adul: (Conversation could not be deciphered)

John: "No, not today. Just two of us. We have to dive. We are coming. It's OK. Many people are coming. Many, many people. We are the first. Many people come."

Adul: "What day?" Their brains were functioning at slow speed. They lost track of the days.

John: "Tomorrow."

Rick: "No, no, no, what day is it?"

John: "Monday. OK, but one week... uh, Monday. You have been here for 10 days. You are very strong."

Ake (in Thai): "Who knows English, translate for us."

Bew (in Thai): "I can't catch up with the words. Slow down."

John: "We'll come."

Adul: "We are hungry."

John: "I know, I know. I understand. We'll come."

Boy 1 (in Thai): "They will take our photos first."

Boy 2 (in Thai): "Tell them we are hungry."

Adul (in Thai) asking the team to exercise patience: "I've told them. They know."

Adul: "What day you come to help me?"

John: "We come here, we have been diving here for what... Tomorrow, we'll help tomorrow. The Navy, Navy SEALs tomorrow. With the food, the doctor and...

Today, a light? You have a light. We'll give you more light."

[Sound of Adul going into the flood water. Bew followed.]

Boy (in Thai): "Come up. Brother, rush up."

John: "That looks fun."

Adul: "I am very happy."

John: "We are happy too."

Adul: "Thank you so much."

John: "OK."
Adul: "Where you come from?"
John: "England, UK."

The undernourished boys, who had lost more than five pounds, were surprised that their saviors were British men who spoke English, and who flew all the way from the United Kingdom to rescue them.

John heaved a huge sigh of relief in what he described as an unprecedented rescue operation.

John and Rick spent some unforgettable moments with the boys, inspiring them to persevere. Not reluctantly, the pair left with mixed emotions but promised to return later with food and medicine.

"We gave them a little bit of extra light. They still had light, they looked in good health. Then, of course, when we departed, all we could think about was how we were going to get them out. So, there was relief, tempered with uncertainty," Rick explained.

23 hours later, torchlights illuminated the water in Chamber Three. Everyone applauded before John and Rick even emerged, completely exhausted. The rescuers relayed the discovery and Narongsak, the commander of the rescue mission, broke the good news to the world who was eagerly waiting to hear.

From then on, it was a race against time. Oxygen levels in the cavern had plunged to 15 per cent against more normal levels of 21 per cent. Medical experts considered 12 per cent a critically low level. The oxygen and carbon monoxide levels were measured by QRAE, a programmable multi-gas monitor for use in hazardous environments.

Further dampening the joyful discovery were the forecasts of more rain. It meant that water levels inside the cave could rise further, making an escape impossible.

With millstones hanging round their necks, the parents of the boys, waiting outside the cave, suddenly went ballistic when they watched their boys came alive on the screen. They looked famished; but otherwise were in pretty good shape despite being stranded in the cave for nine days in near darkness. The spirit of Jao Mae Nang Non had accepted their sacrificial offerings, listened to their earnest prayers and answered them duly.

The once-in-a-lifetime unforgettable encounter was recorded shakily on GoPro cameras mounted on the divers' helmets. It was posted online, which sent millions around the world into wild celebration. They greeted the miraculous news with unbridled joy.

The previously unknown Tham Luang and Mae Sai town were suddenly catapulted into worldwide fame. The boys had no idea what global attention they captured and what coverage they received over their ordeal. An ordinary trip to a cave had transformed them into worldwide celebrities!

A female relative, clutched an iPad showing pictures of some of the boys, had tears of joy streaming down her cheeks as the breaking news flashed on television. She exclaimed, "I'm so happy I can't put it into words."

"I'm so glad. I want him to be physically and mentally fit," exclaimed Tinnakorn Boonpiem, mother of Mark, 13. Her worst fears accumulated over the past nine days proved to be unfounded.

The exhilaration caused by the new-found discovery quickly subsided into doubts and anxiety. It was a one-eighty from joy to despair.

"It's fantastic. It's amazing," remarked Ben Reymenants, "But now the real work starts, how to get them out. That's the real challenge." Ben, a Belgian, ran a dive shop, Blue Label Diving, in Phuket. Besides ocean dives, the shop also conducted cave diving. Ben was believed to be part of the team that first found the boys that Monday.

"After the euphoria of finding the team, the reality set in of the seemingly impossible task ahead: getting them out of the cave," admitted Vern.

"The only thing is that once we found them, we began thinking, now what?" reflected John.

Mikko Paasi and his wife celebrated their eighth wedding anniversary. His wife bought him a timely present - a flight to Chiang Rai to help in the rescue. Mikko, a Finn, was the founder of a diving school on the idyllic Thai island of Koh Tao, where he focused on wreck and cave diving.

With this discovery that commanded worldwide attention, Bill reinforced his team and quickly summoned two additional cave divers, Chris Jewell, 35, and Jason Mallinson, 50. Together with three other divers, they flew to Chiang Rai with new equipment. Chris and Jason were members of Cave Diving Group, Britain's oldest amateur association of subterranean divers. In 2004, Jason was part of the team that rescued six British soldiers trapped for eight days in Alpazat cave in Mexico.

Joining the British team of seven was Tim Acton, 39, who relocated from England to Southeast Asia twelve years ago. Previously a commercial diver, he now ran a holiday complex in Thailand with his wife, Took.

Besides being publicity-shy, the British heroes avoided the media at all costs. John explained single-mindedly on his role, "We've got a job to do."

"I feel it's a long time to wait but it's okay if it makes him safe," Night's sister, Phunphatsa said, "without him, the house is quiet."

Many Thais believed Ake, the assistant coach, was a spiritual force, sent by the Divine to protect the young boys in a past-time that had gone horribly wrong. He coached the boys to meditate and to conserve as much energy as possible until rescue arrived. He warned them against drinking the flood water. Ake was amongst the three weakest as he sacrificed his share of the food earlier.

"If he didn't go with them, what would have happened to my child?" asked the mother of Tee, 16, a defender. "When he comes out, we have to heal his heart. *Pee* Ake, I would never blame you."

However, some quarters put the blame squarely on Ake. Having hiked in Tham Luang on a few occasions, he was acquainted with the monsoon months. Besides, at the cave's entrance, there was a large warning sign in red screaming at visitors - refrain from entering during the raining season.

DAY 11, JULY 3, TUESDAY

The search was successfully completed and the next phase, rescue, kicked in.

Starting at 5 am, seven Thai Navy SEALs and a military medic, Lt. Col. Dr. Pak Loharnshoon, trekked and dived over a mile and a quarter to reach the trapped Wild Boars. They arrived with food, electrolyte drinks, painkillers, antibiotics and oxygen canisters. The boys wrapped themselves with compact and lightweight emergency foil space blankets. They kept the boys warm by reducing heat loss from their bodies.

Because of his rare combination of diving and medical skills, Dr. Pak, 39, was specially handpicked for this commando-like mission. He had graduated from medical school and completed the vigorous Navy SEAL training. His parents, elder brother and wife were all doctors.

When the rescuers arrived, the boys thought they would be freed because the British duo had told them yesterday that the Thai Navy SEALs would be coming today to help them. The Thai Navy SEALs, however, explained that they could not extract them out today.

The famished boys begged for *pad krapao*. This Thai basil chicken dish is one of the most popular Thai street foods. The chicken is stir fried with Thai holy basil, and served with rice and a fried egg. However, on doctor's orders, the thirteen were put on a special diet of medicated liquid food as they had not eaten for the last ten days. PowerGel, comprising of easily digestible carbohydrates combined with sodium, was given to optimize the boys' strength. Restoring the health of the boys was the first priority. Mineral water with added vitamins was also supplied. Surprisingly, the boys only had bruises and minor injuries. Dr. Pak cleaned up the wounds and recorded it to share with the outside world through social media. He also entertained the boys.

To pass their time, the divers played checkers with all the boys except Titan who was afraid to be defeated. The boys lost to a Thai Navy SEAL who dubbed himself 'King of the Cave'. The Thai Navy SEALs dished out advice on how to protect themselves and survive in the cave. One of the boys even regarded one of the Thai Navy SEALs like his father because he called him 'kid'.

"The Thai Navy SEALs always came up with fun activities for us and told us stories," said Pong. "The boys didn't even mind being trapped a bit longer because they'd grown so fond of the SEALs," confessed Ake.

Three Thai Navy SEALs and Dr. Pak stayed with the Wild Boars till the end. Amongst the divers who delivered food to the boys was Jason Mallinson, a British.

Nopparat, head coach of Wild Boars, who was replaced by Ake for that fateful training on Saturday, was surprised, "All of them are very strong physically and mentally. The video clip I saw of them surprised me a lot. I thought they would show some signs of sickness."

Four boys, including Night, Note and Dom, spent their birthdays in the eerie darkness of the cave. They were in no mood to sing Happy Birthday!

Rescuers started to figure how to extract 13 people from the flooded two-and-a-half-mile stretch of rugged caves that even experienced divers struggled in.

"Time is not on our side because they're expecting heavy rains within three days," commented Belgian diver, Ben Reymenants, "They're mentally stable which is actually pretty good."

The overland team led by Surachai Thathet, head of the National Park Rescue, Northern Thailand Unit, narrowed their search on the area around Nern Nom Sao.

To retrieve the boys out by diving, they needed full-faced masks. Water had to be pumped out as well. According to geologist, Chaiporn, there are two streams - Nam Dun Creek to the north and Pak Tin Fai Creek to the south. Water seeped through holes at the bottom of the creeks flooding Tham Luang. Also, when it rained, the water seeped through the porous limestone into the cave. Water from the creeks had to be stopped. Anusorn Intawong, Chiang Rai Rescue Unit Team Leader, was tasked with this assignment. They lifted up rocks to locate the stream sinks and sealed them with sandbags. At the same, water pumps continued to work on overdrive.

DAY 12, JULY 4, WEDNESDAY

The Facebook page of the Thai Navy SEAL showed a photograph of the smiles of the thirteen faces as they spoke to Dr. Phak and his men. The cave-drilling team labored to drill while the water pumping team strained their pumps to drain out the waters. Irrigation officers continued to divert water streams away from the cave's direction.

After two days, the boys regained strength and started to chat more. They were ready to return to their normal lives and had conversation of eating delicious food together.

On the assumption that a rescue would be implemented through the floodwater, the Navy SEALs coached the boys on how to dive and breathe with the diving apparatus. The planning team of cave rescue experts intensified their brainstorming sessions to finalize the best rescue strategy. Oxygen tanks would be positioned at three strategic locations. Each diver had three oxygen tanks strapped to him while pulling another three. Eventually, each diver carried six tanks.

The British team dived to collect more information from the boys in order to map out a detailed rescue plan. It took five hours to get from Chamber Three to Nern Nom Sao where the boys were and back.

The oxygen level had plunged from 21% to 15%. Tubes were laid to pump in more oxygen. However, with the unforgiving terrain, tubes could only reach Chamber Three.

DAY 13, JULY 5, THURSDAY

"How can we help them?"

"One member in our team watched the rescue mission on television," recounted Abdulrawheep Khunraksa, 49, the leader, explaining what triggered his team into the thick of the action at Tham Luang, "We may have the expertise to help since we have climbed cliffs to collect bird's nests for generations."

Libong Island is located in Trang province, southern Thailand. It has a small Muslim fishing community. It is known for its flora, fauna and beaches. Bird's nest collecting has been the main economy for hundreds of years. Although Libong no longer has bird's nests, collectors seek them on other islands and provinces. Bird's nests are harvested three times a year - in February, April and August. Each harvest lasts about seven days. When harvesting for the third time, harvesters wait until the chicks have flown away before they climb up.

These bird's nest harvesters climb steep limestone cliffs with great agility, like mountain goats. They explore crevices and caves to collect bird's nests. The Chinese pay a hefty price for the bird saliva which is the main ingredient for an expensive delicacy – bird's nest soup. Drinking it is believed to give many health benefits.

Friends of the harvesters on the remote island passed the hat around for their air tickets to Chiang Rai.

Bird's nest harvesters from Libong Island searched the cavities

A team of eight, ranging in age from the 20's to 50's, pitted their generations-old rock-climbing skills against time. They swept the mountains for cavities that could possibly lead to the trapped thirteen.

Equipped with only rudimentary ropes, gloves and their intimate knowledge of mountaineering, the team scaled the limestone cliffs hunting for the keyhole to Tham Luang. The dense jungle vegetation hampered their efforts.

Their leader vowed, "We will stay until the mission completes. We will be responsible for all expenses and we don't want to burden anyone."

Thai Navy SEALs transporting oxygen tanks

Taking advantage of the kind weather as the flood receded further, the Thai Navy SEALs expedited the delivery of oxygen tanks and positioned them every 80 feet. A tank of oxygen was insufficient for a diver to reach the boys at Nern Nom Sao. His Majesty, The King of Thailand, sent messages of encouragement to every department and organization.

Dennis Kramer, a 9-year-old Dutch-Thai boy wrote a letter to Prime Minister Mark Rutte of Netherlands to assist. As pumping water out of the cave had little impact, he wrote, "Netherlands is an expert in water management. Can you maybe do something about it? Thanks in advance and friendly greetings." It was unknown if the Dutch Prime Minister responded.

DAY 14, JULY 6, FRIDAY

The cave-drilling team realized that the tunnel they drilled was not near Nern Nom Sao where the boys were trapped.

Since the flood had dropped to an acceptable level, Narongsak decided that evacuation of the thirteen should be executed.

Prince Dipangkorn Rasmijoti, heir presumptive to the throne of Thailand, sent a postcard written in German and dated July 3, encouraging the thirteen trapped youths, "Dear children, I'm sure you're terribly afraid but you're always in my thoughts. I'm overjoyed that you're safe and healthy. I'm also deeply thankful to all helpers who made this rescue successful."

Saman Gunan, 38, a retired Navy SEAL left his airport security job and rushed to join in volunteer rescue efforts. In a fatalistic dive, he transported and placed oxygen tanks on the underwater supply route. The Navy SEALs waited at Chamber Three for 15 hours till 1.30 am when his dive partner returned alone with bad news.

Saman had lost consciousness in an underwater passageway while laying the oxygen tanks. His dive partner failed to revive him. Some Thai officials said he ran out of oxygen in

Saman passed away while laying oxygen tanks

his tanks while others believe he succumbed to hypothermia. It was the rescue mission's first and only casualty. Later in the same day, his funeral rites took place. His family declined an autopsy. Incense was burnt and food was offered as Buddhist monks chanted sutras for Saman's rebirth. His selfless act would help in his afterlife.

"I'm very proud of him but I am very sad, too," mourned Wichai Gunan, Saman's father, a car mechanic. "He is a hero who did all he could to help the boys. Rest well. Daddy loves you."

Waleeporn, Saman's widow, recalled, "He's been praised as a hero because of who he was. He loved helping others, doing charity work and getting things done. Saman once said - we never know when we're going to die, so we need to cherish every day." It is a basic tenet in Buddhism that existence is suffering.

"We will not let Saman's life be in vain. We will carry on. The sacrifice of our friend will not go to waste," swore Rear Admiral Apakorn, "Waleeporn should be proud of her husband. The world sees him as a hero."

"Yesterday I mentioned the real hero was Sam," said Narongsak, "On the day he died, we were very depressed. But we used the sadness to unite us," he said. To save the boys, the Thais believed, a person had to be sacrificed to appease the spirit of Jao Mae Nang Non who resided in the cave. And that sacrificial lamb was Saman. Animal sacrifices were insufficient.

Saman's demise underscored the perilous rescue mission and the risks confronting the boys. Saman was a fit-as-a-fiddle diver who had represented his country in triathlons. The casualty caused an operation pause. The planning team took a step back and reassessed the situation. But it did not slow up the operation. It still had to move forward.

Ratdao Chantapoon, the mother of Note expressed her worry, "The Thai Navy SEAL had practiced for so long and was so strong but he still died. How about a boy who has never dived before?"

Three other Thai Navy SEALs were hospitalized after the oxygen in their air tanks ran low. At times, swift currents pushed divers off-track for hours at a stretch. Sometimes, the strong currents tore off their face masks.

DAY 15, JULY 7, SATURDAY

Phra Khuva Boonchum, The Monk of Three Nations, visited the cave again and repeated the prayers to appease the spirit. Asked about the trapped boys, he predicted, "Don't worry. The boys are safe. They will come out in a few days." His prediction came true.

The boys put on a brave front to reassure their families who were eagerly waiting for them outside the cave. The first page of the note was written by the assistant coach, Ake.

"What we want to communicate: The kids say don't be worried about them. All of them are strong. They would like to eat many different kinds of foods when they come out. Teachers, please don't give them too much homework. The SEALs and doctor Phak, who are taking care of the children, are also well." Ake, 25, the assistant coach.

"I'm fine. It's a little cold here." Dom, 13, striker and captain.

"Father and mother, please don't worry about me. I am fine. Please take me to eat fried chicken after this. I love you," Titan, 11, the youngest, forward

"I love you, father and mother. Don't worry about me. I'm safe now." Pong, 13, left winger. He supported England in the World Cup and was wearing an England jersey.

"I love you, mom and dad. I love you all." Night, 17, right winger.

"I'm safe, please don't worry. I love father and mother and everyone," Note,15, midfielder.

"Mum, are you doing well at home? I am doing well. Please tell my teacher I love her. Love you, mum." Mark, 13, midfielder.

"I love you, mum and dad, and I want to eat barbecue pork." Nick, 15, midfielder.

"Don't worry about me. I miss you all, grandpa, aunt, mother, dad and siblings. I am happy inside here. The Thai Navy SEALs take good care of me. Love you all." Mig, 13, defender.

"I miss you, mom and dad. Don't worry about me. I can take care of myself." Tern, 14, defender.

"Don't worry about me. I hope you all, dad, mum, and siblings, are happy." Tee, 16, defender.

"Don't worry about us now. I miss everyone and I want to go home quickly." Adul, 14, left defender, the only Christian in the group.

"Don't worry about me, dad and mum. I'll be away for just two weeks. I'll help you sell goods, mum, when I have time. I'll rush out of here." Bew, 14, goalkeeper.

"To aunt and grandmother, I'm alright. Do not worry about me. Please take care of yourself. Please prepare vegetable juice and dried pork skin for me. I'll eat it when I'm out. I love all of you." Ake.

"The children are alright. The rescue team is taking good care of them. I promise I will look after your children to the best of my ability. Thank you for your support. I want to also sincerely apologize to all of the parents." Ake in a note to the parents of the boys.

In response, the parents wrote, "*Pee* Ake, we parents would like to ask you to look after our children. Don't blame yourself. We want you to rest assured none of us feels angry with you. We all understand and support you. Thank you for looking after our children. Coach, you've gone in there with them. Come out with them too and do it safely."

Joy, Ake's friend at the monastery, revealed, "I know him, and I know he will blame himself."

"My dear Titan, mummy is waiting for you outside the cave. Mummy loves you and misses you so much. You have to be patient and fight. You have to be strong. I'm waiting for you just outside. You have to make it. I believe you can do it," Titan's mother.

The parents of Adul replied, "Daddy and mummy long to see your face. We pray for you and your friends so we can see you soon. Once you've come out of the cave, we want you to say 'Thank You' to every officer. We want you to trust God and not to worry. Daddy and mummy will be waiting for you until you come out."

Another mother wrote, "You'll always have mummy's support. I love you so much. Daddy also misses you dearly and loves you with all his heart."

DAY 16, JULY 8, SUNDAY

"We, the Thai team and the international team, will bring the Wild Boars home."

The Thai Navy SEAL posted the above message with a rallying photo of interlocking arms on Facebook.

Elon Musk, founder and CEO of Space X, wanted to send a team of expert engineers to assist in the complicated and bold rescue.

The weather was kind to Tham Luang. The muddy flood receded to manageable levels. The physical state of the coach and his footballers was nursed back to normal. Mentally, they were primed to be positive. Narongsak commented, "We have two obstacles: water and time. This is what we have been racing against since day one. We have to do all we can, even though it is hard to fight the force of nature."

He signaled the green light for the massive but intricate rescue operation to commence. "We believe that we will never be as ready as today. If we don't take the chance to make this our D-Day, we could lose a window of opportunity."

The first batch of four boys was rescued.

DAY 17, JULY 9, MONDAY

The divers took five hours to replace the oxygen tanks along the rescue route. The water level was low and there were sufficient men for the rescue. There was no big meeting like in the past and the rescue began at 11 am.

At 8 pm, the second batch of boys was successfully extracted and sent to hospital.

DAY 18, JULY 10, TUESDAY

The last batch was brought out safely. The operation this round went faster than the first two days. At this time on the first day, the boys had not even reached Chamber Two.

The last boy left the now world-renowned cave at 6.47 pm. Over the last 18 days, the world had sat up and googled Tham Luang near Mae Sai, Northern Thailand.

The Thai Navy Seals, Dr. Phak and the international diver teams helped to bring the last batch of boys out. Titan had to cling on to Ake.

"Boss, I did it!" shouted Somkid Mahawongsanun from Pongpa Sub-District, Chiang Rai Province.

Divers and volunteers gave high fives and hugs to each another. All press people and Thais spilled out on the streets of Mae Sai applauding. Motorists blared their horns in a celebratory mood.

The Public Health Permanent Secretary announced that the thirteen were in a good state of health. However, they had lost weight and needed to remain in hospital. Also, they needed to be quarantined in case of any cave diseases caused by bat or bird droppings.

July 11, Wednesday
A Thai military unit dismantled a section of water pumps. They left in an open-topped truck, waving triumphantly to the villagers and the children who remained to bid them a hero's farewell.

July 13, Friday
The Thai Navy SEAL announced it would incorporate cave-diving into its training regimen.

"SEALs need cave-diving training," said Rear Admiral Apakorn on his post-mission priorities for his unit.

In the rescue, "many simply did not know what to do," said Lt Cdr. Khai Tochaiphum, a former Thai Navy SEAL instructor, "none had cave-diving experience."

July 18, Wednesday
The twelve boys and their coach were released from Chiang Rai Prachanukroh Hospital. Accompanied by the Chiang Rai Administrative Organization, they appeared in a press conference – Sending Mu Pa Back Home – at the auditorium at Kochasarn Building.

September 6, Thursday
The Prime Minister, General Prayut Chan-o-cha (Ret.) invited all who were involved in the search and rescue to the 'United as One' banquet at the Royal Plaza, Dusit Palace.

October 6, Saturday
The boys and the coach witnessed the Youth Olympics Opening in Buenos Aires, Argentina.

October 7, Sunday

The boys played against River Plate football club. They drew 3-3.

October 9, Tuesday

Narongsak Osatanakorn, the rescue commander, received the Asia Game Changer Award in New York.

October 15, Monday

The boys and the coach appeared in the Ellen Degeneres talk show. They met Zlatan Ibrahimovic, a Swedish professional footballer who plays as a forward for LA Galaxy in United States.

December 28, Friday

In Britain New Year Honors, Richard Stanton and John Volanthen received the George medal, the second-highest civilian gallantry award. Chris Jewell and Jason Mallinson received Queen's gallantry medals while Vernon Unsworth was awarded a MBE.

PART 3

Mission Impossible

MANPOWER

The foreign rescuers descended from all over world, including England, United States, Canada, Australia, Russia, Sweden, Germany, Italy, Denmark, Czech Republic, Finland, Ukraine, Israel, China, Japan, South Korea, Laos and Singapore. Some volunteered while others were invited by Thai authorities when they acknowledged it was a task of epic proportions.

Thailand mobilized a team of 10,000, consisting of 110 Thai Navy SEALs (Sea, Air and Land teams) divers, police, soldiers, border guards, park officers, government officials and volunteers for its 24-hour rescue mission.

There were representatives from 100 government agencies and state enterprises. At least eleven private companies were involved.

It also involved about 90 divers in all, 50 of them were from abroad and collaborated with Thai Navy SEALs. As the Navy SEALs had no cave-diving experience, it was a monumental challenge.

There was a core team of 18 divers – 13 foreign and 5 Thai Navy SEALs. Among others, the core team consisted of John Volanthen and Rick Stanton from the United Kingdom, Dr. Richard Harris from Australia and Erick Brown from Canada.

The divers battled the elements courageously. Against a strong current, they swam fearlessly. Many a time, the rising, petrifying floodwaters forced a rout.

The divers courted death every time they dived into Tham Luang's twisting and hideous dark tunnels. And, each time, they cheated death by the skin of their teeth.

On 24-hour standby were medics, ambulance drivers, and helicopter pilots to rush the boys straight to Prachanukroh Hospital in Chiang Rai, which was an hour's drive away.

VOLUNTEERS

"We're still seeing the sky but the thirteen in the cave see nothing. We think of them as our kids."

A farmer empathized, watching helplessly as water being pumped out of the cave destroyed his crops and poultry. He added, "Everyone is helping in the mission. This is the way we help. We're glad that the kids are still alive although our land is flooded."

One farmer volunteered to cook for the rescuers, only to find her field flooded upon returning home. "Never mind. The lives of the children are more important."

Another farmer, Sri Tammachoke, was working in the paddy field when the village head announced that the water in the cave would be pumped out into her field. She gave consent. If the water reached the children, they would perish. If the fields were flooded, she could replant the rice. Her heart sank when she saw her crops destroyed; yet she empathized with the trapped kids. The government offered compensation with money and seeds but she refused as they had spent a lot of money already. Additionally, Sri helped to cook and clear rubbish at the cave until 8 am when she returned to work in her paddy field.

Farmers and people in Pong Pha, Si Mueang Chum and Ban Dai's sub-districts of Mae Sae were inundated with the water pumped out of the cave. Farms were destroyed. They accepted it graciously in the spirit of Thai unity and kindness in what appeared to be a national crisis.

Mr. K, owner of a goldsmith shop in Chinatown Bangkok, serving breakfast consisting of coffee, omelet and other snacks.

The restrictions on access to Tham Luang did not stop people from volunteering. Hundreds of villagers cooked food, massaged tired bones, trimmed hair, washed soiled clothes, cleared dirty trash and cleaned over-used toilets for the hundreds of Navy SEALs, divers, rescuers, police officers and park rangers. This extensive support was the oil that lubricated the rescue machinery.

Barbers from Chiang Rai trimming hair for officers and volunteers

Others like Bangkok resident, Thirawit, 44, stepped up as a volunteer translator. He noticed the spirit of empathy circulating in Thailand. "In Mae Sai, nobody is watching the World Cup. Instead, they are watching the rescue operation and counting down on how many have been rescued. This is definitely more exciting than the World Cup."

Shop owner, Sanan, philosophized, "If we can't directly help rescue the boys and their coach, we can help in other ways." On two occasions, he and his team cooked Halal food for a group of 20 bird's nest harvesters from Trang in southern Thailand. A weaver, Nangnoung Namun, volunteered and cooked hundreds of meals a day. She was elated by the rescue, "Now I can sleep peacefully. I'm so relieved." A 23-year-old American tourist changed her travelling plans to volunteer as a cook. She admitted, "I'm glad to see collaboration here. It is difficult to see it in the West."

Cooks whipping out meals for rescuers

Laundry business owner, Rawinmart Luelert, 30, headed to Tham Luang and offered to wash the clothes of rescuers who had toiled for 24 hours. Every day, she washed about 90 pieces of clothing belonging to military, park rangers, divers and specialists.

"I don't have a lot of money to buy things to donate," Rawinmart said. "I cannot cook. But I own a laundromat and I have seen that the personnel's clothes are always dirty with mud." All volunteers who washed dirty clothes for the Navy SEALs were given commemorative SEAL T-shirts.

The owner of a laundry, Miss White, washed dirty linens of soldiers and volunteers round the clock daily

One lady from Chiang Mai took a bus for six hours to Mae Sai so that she could help. Unable to afford a hotel, she lived with a resident.

The mountain park toilets were over-used. Volunteers cleaned the filthy bowls and mopped the dirty floors. Drivers offered free lifts to both volunteers and soldiers. Divers and volunteers whose clothes were soiled with mud had them washed and ironed by local laundromats every day.

Volunteers from Chiang Rai clearing rubbish at Tham Luang's entrance

In Japan, disaster rescue efforts are led by the government. In Thailand, such rescue operations are organized and driven by grassroots communities. Such bottom-up leadership is more disorganized but more inspirational, collaborative and resilient.

Thais, ethnic minorities and foreigners participated in the rescue. It demonstrated teamwork and compassion transcended across all boundaries for the cause of the common good. Many supported each another in the spirit of humanity. It was a brilliant testimony to showcase Thai leadership in managing international teams.

"The selfless giving has been truly extraordinary," blogged Thai social media commentator Kaewmal, "People in the area are generous, helpful, giving and community-minded."

Villagers, united as one, donated money and food packages to the relatives of the boys and their coach. The crisis bonded Thailand into an international symbol of a nation united. Volunteers arrived from other cities in Thailand, by air or road, to lend a hand. Social media was abuzz with messages of love, hope and compassion.

A hive of colorful activities blossomed at the otherwise inconspicuous cave that was overshadowed by dense trees and bushes. The entrapped thirteen footballers triggered Tham Luang to get noticed on the world map. It is now set to be a major tourist attraction in Northern Thailand.

Food stalls mushroomed overnight serving thirst-quenching energy drinks, basil rice with chicken and pork, hot noodles and iced lollipops. The Thai Royal Kitchen even installed mobile kitchens converted from the cargo beds of three army trucks.

The mammoth rescue exercise involved more than 10,000 people. It was a grueling challenge to direct and co-ordinate the various diversed teams. Anyone could volunteer. Those who came with equipment discussed their expertise with the technical teams. The authorities would then assign relevant duties to them.

Overnight, the entire Tham Luang area was transformed to a vibrant tent city.

JOURNALISTS

At least 1600 journalists, both local and foreign, descended on Tham Luang, not counting the hundreds of volunteers who arrived from all over the world. It was every journalist's dream to report a scoop and breaking news. Every small activity led the journalists into a media scrum. The last disaster which had attracted hordes of journalists was four years ago - the missing flight of Malaysia Airlines MH370. The last conference to attract so many journalists was the Trump-Kim Peace Summit held in Singapore June 12, the week prior to the Tham Luang ordeal.

LOGISTICS

The thirteen were deserted on a rocky perch encircled by menacing floodwaters, half a mile deep from the mountain top and two and a half miles from the cave entrance. This fearless rescue operation demanded a humongous amount of both specialized equipment and materials like heavy-duty pumps, oxygen tanks, pulleys, stretchers, wet suits, masks, guide ropes, torches, space blankets and food gels. It also involved drilling machines and complicated electricity and communication cables.

Cave divers always use a reference or guide line when they first swim into a cave. The line is unspooled from a reel as they dive further into the cave. It is tied to rocks where possible. The divers can then follow this guide line in and out of the cave. With this line, additional stronger ropes can be installed. In the murky waters of Tham Luang with near zero visibility, they could hold on and navigate with the guide line. Even if they lost their masks, they could find their way by feeling along the rope.

Rope pulley systems were installed at the cave roof. Green SKED stretchers encasing the boys could be hoisted up, turned and transported swiftly above the craggy rocks.

The divers wore improvised equipment held together with heavy-duty duct tape.

While His Majesty, the King of Thailand donated supplies generously, ordinary Thais from all walks of life volunteered by whipping up meals, snipping hair, massaging tired backs and washing soiled clothes for the rescuers. Some operated pumps to suck and drain out the flood water. Yet others searched for hidden holes in the limestone mountain that could lead to the stranded boys.

Over a hundred volunteer chefs whipped up 4,000 to 5,000 packs of food daily from donated fruits, vegetables, fish, meat and rice.

"No one really had any idea what to do," one volunteer said. Villagers in Mae Sai brought along whatever tools and equipment they could lay their hands on – knives, shovels, crowbars, hoes, pails, ropes, pipes, portable water pumps, table and chairs – however insignificant they appeared to be. Some dug into their own pockets to pay for these.

SUPPLIES

Precious food like Dever energy gel, fresh water, and medical supplies like paracetamol and gauze were delivered the day after the boys were found. Food was needed for the boys to build up their energy and nutrient levels.

"The boys were given easy-to-digest, high-energy food with vitamins and minerals, under the supervision of a doctor," explained Rear Admiral Arpakorn.

TELECOMMUNICATION

Tham Luang is situated between mountains. It is a blind spot for communication signals, making co-ordination challenging and delaying the rescue. The five telephone networks were asked to turn their signals towards the cave entrance and increase their mobile bandwidth. Telephone lines were set up inside the cave. However, the thick walls and flooding blocked the radio signals. Two Israeli technology firms assisted by providing communication links in the cave.

Wireless communication was passed through a string of Max-Mesh mobile professional radio devices in places that regular radios would not work, especially when there were major obstacles blocking the line-of-sight between the two ends of the line. In the cave, Maxtech Networks connected the boys to the rescue base by data, voice and video.

"It was like a daisy-chain," explained Uzi Hanuni, CEO of Maxtech. It was like a beacon being lit on one hilltop after another, sending the message in a relay. It took 19 of the devices to complete the link between the boys and the rescuers. Its battery power lasted for 10 hours.

"It is a very complex scenario inside the cave," Hanuni explained.

Some sections snake through twisted passageway for half a mile while others are also submerged in rainwater. For these challenging sections, data cables were installed.

Asaf Zmirly, an Israeli who runs a rescue team in Thailand, was involved in the early stages of the rescue. He contacted Hanuni. Two days later, on Monday, June 25, Maxtech employee Yuval Zalmanov, a senior software engineer, took the next flight to Bangkok-Chiang Rai, bringing the equipment in a suitcase.

"We are happy to be able to help," said Hanuni.

Following their success here, Maxtech wants to establish an emergency team that can respond quickly to disasters in other foreign lands.

A second Israeli tech company, Radwin, which provides point-to-point broadband wireless solutions, donated its wireless equipment to assist in the rescue mission shortly after it was announced.

Led by a local Thai, Thanadon Mankong from its Bangkok office, a team swiftly established the wireless network infrastructure. It enabled the coordination of rescue operations by the large number of forces on the grounds outside the cave where there was little or no connectivity.

While Radwin's tech provided a form of emergency communication, it was not used inside the cave system to help find the boys. According to Ofer Nager, Radwin's general manager in North Asia, the company established a wireless network to help the extensive number of forces on the ground to communicate. With flooding and heavy usage, electrical fibers in the earth and cellular networks in towers were under stress.

In 2004, Radwin donated communication equipment to Thailand during the Indian Ocean tsunami. It was also used to assist the rescue of 33 miners trapped in a San Jose copper mine in Chile in August 2010, as well as during Super Typhoon in the Philippines in November 2013.

Other communication equipment used were:

Heyphones provided by Derbyshire Rescue Organization. This was a low frequency radio that could transmit calls hundreds of feet through solid rock.

The US Army TA-312/PT Field Telephone has been the workhorse field phone of the US Army since it was first introduced in the 1950's.

The Switchboard SB-22 is a small portable field-type telephone switchboard. Hand generators powered the phones to ring the board. The last two were used in the Vietnam War.

PRAYERS

"Please protect the 13 kids."

Tum Kantawong, the godmother of Ake prayed earnestly. Every morning, she gingerly trekked up the mountain paths to offer fruits, incense and candles. She explained, "It was to show respect to the spirit that protects the cave."

Amidst the haste and the noise in the cliff-hanger, many Thais and foreigners alike uttered prayers silently, seeking assurance and safety from the spirits dwelling in the cave.

The boys' families did likewise, asking for blessings from the Divine. The boys' classmates organized group prayers, sang songs aloud into the cave, folded paper cranes and posted messages of love and hope on school noticeboards. Teachers joined in.

"We wanted to be the first to welcome the boys when they came out," said school administrator Ampin Saenta who was regarded as a 'mama-teacher' to Adul.

Many Thais throughout the whole world followed the news closely and prayed for freedom for the trapped boys. One was Boat, a Thai working for Reuters in Singapore. Like the rest of his countrymen who love visiting caves, he had visited Tham Yai Nam Nao cave in North East Thailand before. The first 1600 feet was a tourist area – spacious, safe and illuminated with lightbulbs. When he hiked further in, he descended into a dark, narrow and depressing passage scattered with potholes. A river ran under the cave. So, Boat could empathize with what the Wild Boars were experiencing.

FAKE NEWS

"The boys' bodies would float out of the cave entrance."

Ikan Wiboonroongruang, whose 11-year-old son Titan was the youngest of the trapped boys, was very distraught by this rumor. Although she was prepared for the worst, rumors were adding unnecessary fuel to the already tense atmosphere.

As the world demanded more updates, unidentified persons appeared at the cave's surroundings and dished out information. Inaccurate news caused confusion among the rescuers and volunteers, affecting the operations. They also caused undue worry to the already stressed families and relatives of the boys. The rumors spread rapidly too. As if the rescue operation was not stressful enough, Narongsak had to correct the fake news too.

Fake news surfaced randomly: the thirteen sought shelter in the cave because it was raining; they entered the cave to celebrate a boy's birthday; they brought party food along with them; they could not swim; they had been the cave a few times; etc.

DANGERS AT THAM LUANG

There were many dangers lurking at Tham Luang where a visitor could become completely isolated. There was no GPS, no Wi-Fi nor mobile phone service.

When the search began, the divers had a rude shock. The estimates of distances between key points were grossly inaccurate and the location of landmarks suspect. The last known survey was conducted in the 1980's by a French caving society but many of its deepest recesses remained unmapped. Spelunkers considered Tham Luang one of the most challenging caves in the world.

Many basic assumptions were wrong. There were too many variables and unknowns in the cavern – pitch-darkness, flood levels, strength of currents, duration of rain, oxygen levels, rough terrain, narrow passages, the boys' health, their mental strength etc. – to be factored in the rescue that made it life-endangering to conduct.

Hypothermia
The thirteen risked hypothermia - when a body dissipates more heat than it absorbs. Hypothermia occurs when the human body's core temperature goes below 95.0 °F. In mild hypothermia, a

victim experiences shivering and mental confusion. To overcome it, the victim must be provided with warm drinks and clothing, and get involved in physical activity. The atmosphere in the cave was damp. Ake shepherded the twelve to a small rock ledge locked in by the flood. He had the presence of mind to get the boys to huddle together to keep dry and warm.

In addition, the damp atmosphere in the enclosed environment, unhygienic living conditions and improper discharge of excrement were ideal conditions for bacteria to propagate and spread.

Oxygen

For a while, there was also enough air. The porous limestone and cracks in the rocks permitted air to flow through.

Then the level of oxygen available in the air at Nern Nom Sao plunged to 15%. The normal level in the atmosphere is 21%. Multi-gas monitors were used to measure the oxygen levels.

To reduce the amount of carbon dioxide they exhaled, officials limited the number of rescue workers in the cave. Non-essential workers were withdrawn. Engineers installed a pipe line to pump in fresh air but it stopped at Chamber Three due to logistical limits. Rescuers transferred about 100 oxygen tanks to the cave to help improve the air supply.

Fresh Rain

The inclement weather was merciless. Heavy rainfall continued to bombard the cave relentlessly. The water levels rose and chambers were flooded, cutting off rescuers completely from inner parts of the cave. Flood waters also assaulted from another entrance at the Monk's series towards the fork junction at Sam Yaek.

When it rained, run-offs swept mud into the cave, causing the water to be muddy. When divers stepped on the floor, it disturbed the sediment and caused it to rise like clouds. This reduced visibility, making it challenging to dive forward. Run-offs also brought along debris which clogged the passages.

Fresh rain brought flood level up to divers' chins

"I don't know of any other rescue that put the rescuer and the rescue in so much danger over a prolonged period of time, unless it is something along the lines of firefighters going into the World Trade Centre knowing that the building was on fire and was going to collapse," reflected Major Hodges.

<u>Options</u>
How to get them out?

The high-level rescue committee led by Narongsak Osottana-korn returned to the drawing board and went into overdrive to generate alternatives and decide on the safest options.

Initially, the boys were fed high-protein gels. Later, they took more normal food. They started to put on a little weight before the evacuation.

<u>Staying</u>

The initial plan was to wait out the monsoon season that ends in November.

"The boys and their coach might have had to stay in the cave for four months until the rainy season subsided," suggested Captain Anand Surawan, deputy commander of the Thai Navy SEAL who was running an operations center.

"The original plan was to keep the thirteen inside the cave for a month or more while rescuers found a way to bring them out, perhaps through another entrance or until the water levels drop," related Rear Admiral Apakorn.

Retaining the boys in the cave for four months was equally risky as oxygen levels had plunged to 15%. If it dropped further to 12%, the boys could fall into a coma.

"That made us worry a lot," confessed Rear Admiral Apakorn. "It was hard to fight nature. What would we do if the oxygen kept decreasing?"

Moreover, diseases were likely to break out in a moist enclosure like a cave. Hygiene standards would be compromised because of poor sanitation and lack of clean water. "It is very likely that infections would have started setting in and the boys would have deteriorated a lot faster than they already had," said Claus Rasmussen, a Danish national, who had lived for years in Thailand. He worked as an instructor with Ben Reymenants. He had been diving across Asia.

"Rescuing the boys through flood was definitely the scariest option," Rasmussen said. They tried to avoid this option. Rescuers would have to carry and pull the boys on SKED stretchers through two and a half miles of tunnels.

"The boys weren't going to stay alive in the chamber. But if you try a risky operation and they die, would it have been better to leave them there and hope the waters go down?" asked Bill Whitehouse, vice chairman of the British Cave Rescue Council.

DOI NAN NON
HEIGHT:4557 FT
DRILLING MACHINE
PAK TIN FAI CREEK
BIRD NEST HARVESTER
SEARCH AND RESCUE DOG
NAM DAN CREEK
WATER SEEPS THROUGH
POROUS LIMESTONES
DEPTH
2700-3300 FT
HOLES
27 FT WIDE 10 FT HIGH
1/4 MILE
FORK JUNCTION
AT SAM YAEK
CHAMBER 3
OXYGEN TANKS
MONK'S SERIES
45° SLOPE
CAVE CONTINUES
TO LAB LAE
12 BOYS AND
THEIR COACH
STRANDED
PATTAYA BEACH
CHOKE POINT
5 FT WIDE
RESCUE DRIVERS
NERN NOM SAO
RESCUE COMMAND
CENTER
DRY BUT MUDDY AREA
WATER PUMP
1.2 MILE
NERN NOM SAO TO SAM YAEK
CHAMBER 2
THAM LUANG
ENTRANCE
WATER PUMP
AMBULANCE
HELICOPTER
13 MEDICAL TEAMS
THAM SAI THONG ENTRANCE
DISTANCE FROM NERN NOM SAO
TO ENTRANCE: 2.5 MILES
TOTAL LENGTH OF CAVE: 6 MILES

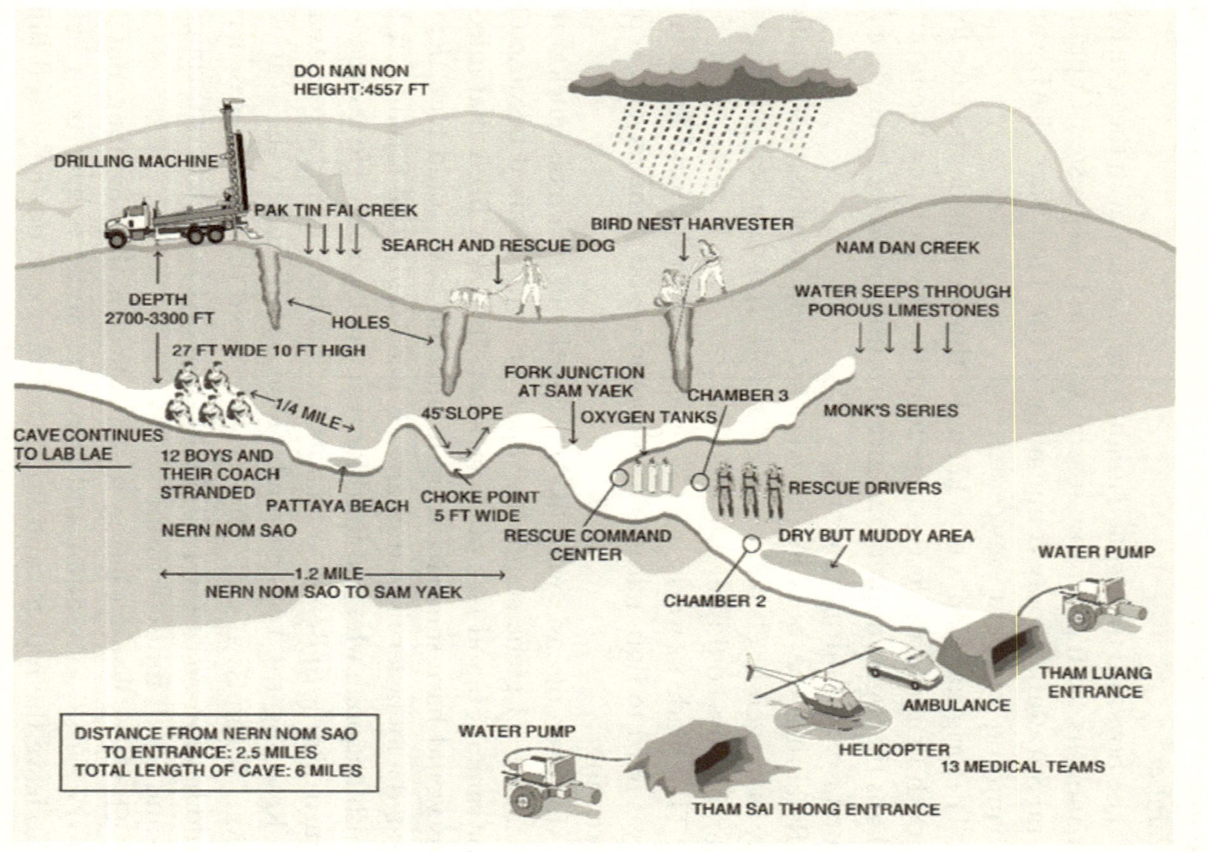

Rescue plan

DRILLING

This strategy comprised of searching out or drilling alternative passages into the cave. Engineers were searching for a spot on the mountain where they could drill down and reach the cave tunnel. The boys could then be hoisted up like the 33 Chile miners.

On 5th August, 2010 there was a cave-in at a copper-gold mine in Atacama Desert in Chile. It trapped 33 men who survived 2,300 feet underground for 69 days. All were successfully rescued on 13th October 2010 over 24 hours. More than 1 billion people worldwide watched the rescue live on television.

Engineers admitted drilling at Tham Luang would take months. It was estimated that the cave depth was more than half a mile. In so doing also, the landscape of both the mountain and the cave might be altered.

New roads leading to the mountains and a solid base to anchor the heavy drilling machines would have had to be constructed. Alternatively, Chinook helicopters could hoist up the machines to a mountain top which would have to be cleared. To pinpoint the exact location amidst a dense jungle and muddy grounds, where the drill could reach the boys, a detailed survey would need to be commissioned. The present maps were sparse in details. The engineers were clueless about which spot to start drilling. "It was like finding a needle in an ocean," lamented Arpakorn. Heavy drilling could disintegrate the rocks causing them to collapse and block passageways in the cave.

They even tried drilling into the mountainside, desperate to find cracks in the cave system through which they could squeeze, and they used drones with thermal sensors to detect possible access points to the boys. More than 100 such shafts were drilled.

"Some of the shafts were as deep as a quarter of a mile but we still could not find their location yet," Narongsak recalled. "Our mission lacked the technology to pinpoint where the boys were."

PUMPING AND DRAINING WATER

Another alternative was to pump water out from the cave and wait for the flood to recede naturally. This could take four months to November.

However, the rising floods gave the pumping more urgency.

"Support teams needed to drain water as fast as possible. So, we had to obtain as many pumps as we could," said General Anupong Paochinda, the Interior Minister.

High-tech industrial-scale pumps were summoned into the disaster zone. Water-drainage teams with powerful pumps arrived from Samut Sakhon's Ban Phaeo district and Nakhon Pathom province. The Czech Republic provided highly efficient pumps – each pump could drain 100 gallons of water per second.

In total, nineteen high-powered pumps were in operation. It was a battle between man-made machinery versus the elements of nature. "The mission was a race against the water," analyzed Narongsak.

Super-turbo giant industrial water pumps

"But the pumps only helped to draw an inch or two of water each day," explained Rear Admiral Apakorn. This was despite the fact that the pumps operated 24 hours each day.

"The problem is there is not enough power if we are running many pumps at the same time," said Thai fireman, Poonshak Wonjsangiam.

According to Narongsak, some unregistered volunteers accidentally pumped water back in the direction of the cave. The excess murky floodwater was funneled into nearby farms, streams and hastily dug wells. It destroyed farms, its produce and poultry.

Although water was pumped out, even more returned, fed by sinkholes and up-streams in the mountains. More monsoon rain threatened to worsen the flood. Not only was probability high, it was imminent.

It the meantime, efforts to pump water out bore some results. As water and mud receded, jagged outcroppings bared their teeth. The waterlogged muddy passageway which took five hours to navigate previously now only required two hours.

The soldiers tried to drill holes in the cave walls to help drain some of the flood water. However, the stubborn, hard rock ensured their efforts were futile.

The great cave, Tham Luang, appeared as a patient undergoing major surgery in the Intensive Care Unit. Long tubes ran through its body and sprouted out of its mouth. The cave entrance was transformed into a quagmire of thick, soggy, orangey-colored paste.

FLOOD DIVERSION

Weirs or low-head dams made of wood and bamboo, were constructed horizontally across the width of the mountain creeks leading to Tham Luang. They diverted the flow of water to other areas. A temporary dam made of bamboo and wood was also erected around the cave entrance to keep rainwater at bay.

The cave cavities were surveyed. Water channels were being diverted away from the cavities.

"The Thai authorities took a lot of steps to divert rivers on the mountaintop which we believe bought us as lot of time to get this outcome," explained Rear Admiral Arpakorn.

Prime Minister Prayut Chan-o-cha requested Myanmar to help block water flowing into Tham Luang, which is located near the Thai-Myanmar border.

*Weirs, like this, were constructed to prevent the flood
water from flowing into the cave*

MINI-SUBMARINE

Tech entrepreneur Elon Musk designed a kid-sized submarine to bring the boys out. Named Mu Pa, it was made of rocket parts. It was rejected as it could not maneuver through the tight passageways.

One of the challenges with Musk's design was that the submarine was a rigid piece of equipment.

Cave passages are seldom straight and wide. If there is a U-bend, it would be difficult for divers to navigate the submarine through it. It is akin to moving a long sofa through a tiny apartment. It is even worse if it is dark with low oxygen levels.

The ideal equipment would be flexible enough to navigate the jagged edges of the walls, and the narrow and twisted passages with low ceilings.

DIVING

"The British were doing the push-ahead and laying down the guidelines for others to follow," said Bill Whitehouse, vice-chair of the British Cave Rescue Council. "It was completely restricted with very dark tunnels and poor conditions, mud banks and areas that needed excavating., They pushed forward on each dive, laying lines and clearing the way."

Thai Navy SEALs followed. They transported and positioned oxygen tanks along the passageway so that the divers could stay longer inside. Meanwhile, the Thai Navy SEALs coached the boys on how to dive in case heavy flooding demanded that they be rescued immediately. Contrary to initial press reports, all the boys could swim, although only a handful were strong swimmers. Moreover, the flood water was cold and muddy.

"If you placed your hand in front of you, it just disappeared," said Kaew, the Thai Navy SEAL who escaped the final deluge. "You couldn't see anything."

There were also narrow passageways to contend with. Even for experienced divers, the six-hour journey presented a risky challenge. The death of a retired Thai Navy SEAL further depressed the gloomy outlook.

In this rescue scenario, fraught with risks, the boys would be escorted by at least two divers. They had to brave strong currents. Inside the narrow passageway, the divers would have to dismount their tanks and wriggle the boys through. In the fully-flooded sections, the boys would need to be transported underwater at near-freezing temperatures for two hours.

Under heavy pressure, the decision-makers cracked their heads on the best alternative.

According to Ruengrit, a Thai diver who coordinated the various diving teams from different countries, diving was the most likely option. On the tense evening of Thursday, July 5, the initial decision was to ferry the boys out escorted in a buddy system by two expert divers - one leading the way and another at the rear or on the side. The operation was supported by a daisy chain of rescuers, waiting to transport boys to the field hospital.

Dr. Harris dived in to assess the boys' health and accompanied them for three days. With his consent, the rescue plan kicked in. If the boys were too feeble, a daring rescue would prove disastrous.

In the meantime, the divers rehearsed the rescue in a nearby swimming pool. Local village boys were only too delighted to volunteer as the trapped boys. During practice, they were transported in the SKED stretchers in the pool by the divers – one in front and one at the back.

The morning of Saturday, July 7, was forecasted to rain heavily. It would flood and block the cave, denying any escape attempt. When the rain took absence of leave and presented a golden window of opportunity, the Thai Navy SEALs knew they must move in swiftly and seize it.

"We had enough people to run the teams, the environment was right, we had a window with the weather," said Rasmussen. "We thought, this is going to be the best option we're going to get. But with the forecast of heavy rains, and the risk of water levels rising, an operation was launched on Sunday, July 8, to bring them out."

THE DECISION

Every morning at 8.30, the select brotherhood of international divers assembled and held meetings with the Thai navy commanders. The planning by the Thai military was meticulous and carefully thought through. "I've never seen anything that's so precise or to the point," said Erick from Canada.

On the weekend, the cave conditions were fast deteriorating. The rescuers were ready to execute the daring rescue for two reasons. One, the forecast read that heavy rain was imminent. Two, the oxygen levels where the boys were marooned had plunged critically to 15% and might even decline to a lethal level of 12%.

The operation strategy changed regularly as each variable fluctuated: the water levels, the mud, the strength of the tide, oxygen levels, as well as the physical and mental state of the thirteen. As none of the boys had experience in diving, they needed full-face masks with oxygen feed.

The diving option was extremely dangerous but the priority was to extract the boys before the monsoon brought more water and debris into the cave. The light rain and the draining of water brought the flood to its lowest level.

D-DAY

Sunday, July 7. The boys had been in the cave for 14 days. All of a sudden, the Thai authorities announced that they were extracting the boys. The monsoon rain that had pelted Mae Sai had petered out, giving the divers a sliver of opportunity to engineer a do-or-die rescue.

"There is no other day that we are more ready than today," declared Narongsak, the commander of the rescue operations. "In the next three or four days, the conditions will be perfect for evacuation in terms of the water, the weather and the boys' health."

"We have to make a clear decision on what we can do. We cannot wait too long because of the rain forecast this week. The water levels from the cave entrance to Chamber Three - where the rescue base is - is currently low enough for personnel to walk through."

"It got to a point where we knew that the weather forecast wasn't going to be too brilliant," Vern predicted, "We said we have to get in."

Local villagers pre-warned the commanders that by July 10 every year, the cave would be flooded completely.

The boys had been given high-protein and high-energy food. Narongsak added, "They can communicate clearly, and joke and play among themselves."

Meanwhile, the Australian government negotiated immunity for its divers with the Thai government in case the rescue resulted in injuries or worse, deaths.

Both journalists and volunteers were ordered to vacate the cave rescue site and relocate their base 1500 feet further down so that the rescuers could remain totally focused on the task at hand.

The incredible rescue began involving nearly 100 Thai and foreign divers. Inside the cave, the innocent boys were ignorant of the real dangers ahead. They actually looked forward to diving. On the contrary, the divers were burdened with many anxious moments. "There were way too many unknowns," said Rasmussen, a Danish volunteer diver.

The flood level from Chamber Three to the fork junction at Sam Yaek to Nern Nom Sao where the boys were trapped was still high.

"During the peak of the rainy season, we are worried that the area where the boys are will be inundated or reduced to just 100 square feet," Narongsak confessed his concern as he evaluated the different options. There was also a possible rise in carbon dioxide and a corresponding drop in oxygen in the cave. Rescuers managed to establish a line to pump in fresh air. Non-essential workers were withdrawn to conserve the oxygen levels inside.

Saman's death only occurred a day earlier. The divers were dicing with death every time they plunged into the flood.

MASKS

"Anyone trying to buy a scuba mask in Thailand this week would be disappointed. Basically, every full-face mask in the country is here," cautioned Changkwanyuen, a Thai diver who helped coordinate the diving teams. He placed orders for large quantities of patented Ocean Reef full-face masks, each costing USD 900, just in case some of them failed. He also organized the delivery of equipment like small wetsuits and underwater lights.

Full-face masks would enable the boys to experience natural breathing through the nose. There is no jaw fatigue as there is nothing to bite on, thus freeing the mouth. They are anti-fog. There is flooding as the breathing automatically drain the water away.

Bill from the British Cave Rescue Council also sourced kid-sized full-face diving masks and some harnesses from a French firm. One British supplier drove from shop to shop to secure what masks were left.

The masks the US team brought with them were adult-sized. By pulling the five straps as tight as possible, they would work. However, one of the boys could not be extracted on the first two days because there was no full face mask small enough for him.

SKED STRETCHER

The US team, comprising of 30 members, recommended that each boy be confined in a SKED.

The **SKED** stretcher is a shock-proof, durable and yet flexible proven system for a confined space, high-angle or technical rescue. It is a plastic cocoon-like stretcher and protects the boy like what a tray does for an egg.

Made in Austria with a special plastic formula, its Cobra side-release steel buckles are reliably strong and yet, easy to use. Under tension, they are very difficult to release. So accidental release is out of the question. When the patient is packaged, the plastic stretcher becomes rigid. It offers secure protection when evacuation takes place even in the most demanding environment. The **SKED** is equipped for horizontal hoisting by helicopter or vertical hoisting in caves. Surprisingly, it can be rolled for storage in a backpack, and it folds like a yoga mat. A patient can be packaged in a **SKED** stretcher within 60 seconds. A **SKED** stretcher costs $700 apiece.

*SKED stretchers could be carried, hoisted or placed
on a float on the flood water*

The SKED stretchers were versatile. They could be strapped to a diver. They could slide down the hoses for the water pumps which function as impromptu slides. Rope pulleys could suspend the SKED so they can be transported above jagged rocks. In one flooded section, the SKED stretchers could be placed on rafts which the divers push forward.

How Were the Boys Selected?
Initially, Dr. Harris decided that the weakest boys should be extracted first. Later, he reconsidered, "Everyone was equally strong – so they picked among themselves to see who would come out first." Only with his consent could the rescue commence. Dr. Harris gave the rescue a 60-70% chance of success with three to five casualties.

"Who want to leave first?" asked the Navy SEALs for volunteers. None of the boy raised their hands. "No one rushed to get out of the cave because we were so close to one another," explained Ake on their kindred spirit.

The SEALs and Dr. Park consulted with Ake on who to be rescued first.

"Ake, you make the decision," requested the SEALs. Ake was placed in the driver's seat to decide on the sequence in which the boys would dive out.

"The ones whose homes are the furthest will go first, so they can tell everyone that the boys are fine," decided Ake.

Innocent as they were, they thought they would simply grab their bicycles, buy some food and cycle home to face the wrath of their parents. They were unaware that there was a huge crowd looming outside the cave, craning their necks to witness the historic moment, while the entire world stayed tuned to the outcome of this heart-stopping rescue live. Two helicopters and thirteen ambulances, one for each Wild Boar, were waiting impatiently for them at the footsteps of the cave.

Following this, Ruengrit said rescuers planned to start with the strongest boy. As done with the 33 coal miners who were trapped in Chile in 2010, the strongest were to be rescued first. This was to give a ray of hope to the remaining trapped ones so that they would stay strong and be determined to get out alive.

The order of this rescue was not based on strength as observed in standard rescue operations. Instead it was decided by the boys themselves. Naïve as it seemed, the sequence was based on the distance from the cave to their homes.

Ake wrote the order down: 1, 2, 3, 4, 5, 6, 7, 8, 9, 10, 11 and 12." As a true servant-leader, he completed the list:

13 - Ake.

SEDATION

The complexities of cave diving through dangerous passageways was terrifying for experienced cave divers, let alone the boys. Sedation, through injection of anti-anxiety medication, ensured the boys did not panic. For the first time, they would wear strange diving equipment. To make it worse, they would be transported in pitch darkness and icy-cold swirling floods. Sedation would reduce any long-term psychological damage because the boys would not be able to recall the actual rescue.

If they ever panicked, the lives of the divers would be endangered, too. Dr. Harris prepared them for the sedative Ketamine which induced a trance-like state while providing pain relief and memory loss. The sedation lasted between 45 minutes to an hour. Dr Harris had trained divers stationed along the rescue path to re-sedate the boys during the three-hour journey.

Prime Minister Prayuth Chan-o-cha said the boys were lightly sedated. On the contrary, others claimed that the boys were heavily sedated and were only semi-conscious. Rescuers would not comment on its strength.

"If they were anxious, they would squirm," explained Rear Admiral Apakorn, "Some were conscious and some slept. There was no problem. We had to use the means that ensured the children would not be panicky while we were carrying them out."

He added, "It was a joint decision." Given that other observers may disagree, the rescue plan was kept secret so that the rescuers would not be distracted.

At the end of the operation, he concluded, "Most importantly, they are alive and safe."

"They just had to lay there and be comfortable," said Major Hodges, leader of the US team.

Commander Chaiyananta Peeranarong, who oversaw the transfer of the thirteen between Chambers Three and Two, described them all as "sleeping" on the harrowing journey out. "We just needed them to know how to breathe and not panic in the water," he noted.

THE DARING RESCUE OPERATIONS

Day 16, Sunday, July 8 morning. Mission impossible began. A team of 18 audacious divers - 13 foreign divers accompanied by five Thai Navy SEALs - stepped into the cave at 10 am Bangkok time to stage a fearless rescue operation that would keep the world on the edge. They were called the United Nations team. The British Cave Rescue Council suggested who should be in this team. The Thai Navy SEALs left the decision to them as they were not experts in this area.

Through the previous night, the pump operators managed to reduce the water levels by 15 inches.

The original plan was for two divers to extract each boy. It was revised to one diver to one boy. Nine more divers were stationed strategically along the route to support them. Dr. Harris gave the boys a medical sign-off before they jumped off the now-famous Nern Nom Sao mound for the last time to face the unknown waters ahead.

Dr. Harris instructed the divers, "No matter what happens, get them out as fast as possible. Hypothermia is going to be a big issue here."

The boys were split into groups of four. Each boy was guided by one diver, who carried their oxygen tanks and guided them through the murky tunnels. Each rescue took several hours, with much of the time spent underwater.

While the boys were shuttled out, the Navy SEALs, Lt. Col. Dr. Pak, and Dr. Harris stayed with the remaining boys for three days.

At 1 pm, the divers began their dive from Chamber Three for the daring rescue. This might be the last time they saw the boys and their coach alive. The rescue journey was divided into two segments:

First Segment

The first segment was from Nern Nom Sao where the boys were trapped, through Pattaya Beach to Chamber Three, the rescue base. The first segment was the riskier of the two. Although more than 64 million gallons of water (equivalent to 100 Olympic-sized swimming pools) were pumped out, divers had to dive through the remaining flood in total darkness at bone-chilling temperature. At the narrowest gaps, the divers navigated the boys through carefully to avoid dislodging their full face mask against rocks. Imagine navigating in the S-trap in the toilet bowl. Divers kept their heads higher than the boys. In poor visibility the diver would hit their head against the rocks first. The boys' oxygen masks also faced the risk of being ripped off by the strong currents.

"The main challenge is the water which keeps flowing in all the time. This makes the current strong and the water murky," revealed a Thai Navy SEAL.

The boys were kitted with 0.2 inch-thick wetsuits and fitted with full face breathing masks which made it easier for them to breathe underwater compared to scuba gear. Full-face masks reduced the time required to teach the thirteen how to dive. Masks of the right size were critical. There were two choices – the boys could dive or come out as a package. They chose the latter.

John revealed that the divers practiced the rescue technique in a pool with volunteer Thai boys from a local swimming club.

Each boy was clipped to their diver so that they would not be lost in the muddy flood. An oxygen tank was strapped at the front of each boy while a handle was attached to his back of his vest. He was held face down so that water flowed away from his face. The diver adjusted the boy's weight for neutral buoyancy for safety. If the boy floated too much, he would hit the ceiling. If he sank too low, he would hit the jagged rocks.

The divers were guided through the dark by a guide rope which could swing from left to right of the cave. With one hand gripping the guide rope, the other hand held on the handle on back of the boy's vest. Depending on the oncoming hazards, the diver would switch the boy from side to side. The diver moved slightly ahead. In case there was a wall in front, he would take the knock first. The scene was like dancing in a choreographed underwater ballet.

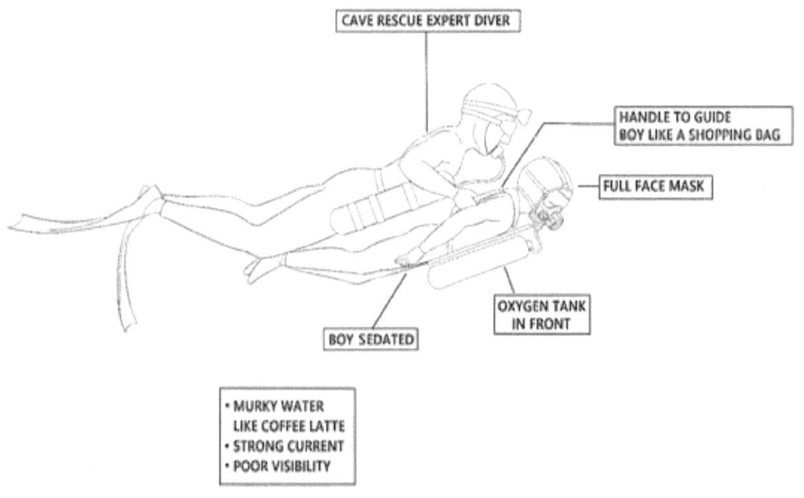

Diver guided the boy like shopping bag

"We strapped a cylinder to the front of the child and they had a full-face mask on. Essentially, we had a handle on the back of the child," he explained, "If you want a picture, it was probably more like a shopping bag that you would sometimes hold close to your chest if the passage was narrow and deep. If the passage was low and wide you would hold them out to the side and essentially maneuver them around any obstacles that were in the way."

The first dive was 1400 to 1700 feet. It took more than two hours. At the narrow passageways - the narrowest being five feet - divers had to unstrap their air tanks to squeeze through, while also carrying along their valuable luggage – the boys. Sometimes, they could not see the rocks until their faces hit them. The divers could see the boys were breathing from their exhaust bubbles.

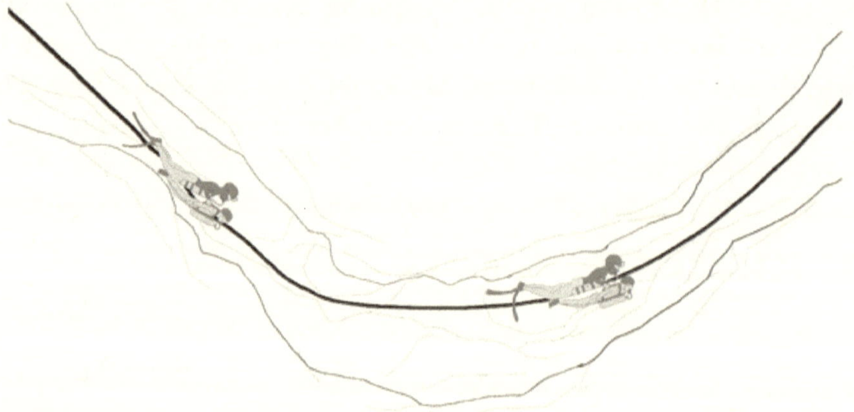

Diver, holding the back of the boy, was guided by guide ropes in the dark

"The last couple of hundred yards underwater is very difficult to find your way through. For the entire dive at the back of the cave, there's zero visibility due to mud and clay. So, you're following the guide line with your hand and you basically might as well have your eyes closed with a small boy being cradled in your arms and feeling your way through rocks and posting yourself sideways through little holes," explained Craig.

After the first dive, the boy was met by three divers. With his dive gear was removed, he was then transported on a SKED stretcher over 700 feet of mud and craggy rocks. Then he was re-kitted with the dive gear and re-submerged for the next under water section. The last section leading to Chamber Three was 1000 to 1400 feet. It was estimated that the dive would take five hours.

A quarter of a mile away stood Pattaya Beach. It was the longest dry patch between Nern Nom Sao, where the boys were trapped and Chamber Three, the key base for the rescue operation.

Second Segment

The second segment was from Chamber Three to the entrance.

After passing through the first segment, they arrived at Chamber Three, the rescue base, at 45 minutes interval. Although no more diving was necessary, the remaining journey to the entrance was still laden with risks.

Upon emerging, a doctor would check each boy's temperature, blood pressure, pulse, oxygen level and skin color. Next, he was transferred to a SKED stretcher where he was securely fastened. Each stretcher was carried by rescue teams of six each. More than a hundred rescuers were stationed strategically at regular intervals along this section. This included nurses who checked on the boys who were in a semi-conscious state.

"We didn't want the children to walk because it is really tiring to get from Chamber Three to the cave mouth," Rear Admiral Apakorn said. "We brought the children out like eggs protected in stone." He was referring to the Thai idiom about parents being overprotective of children.

Rescuers transporting the boy

Many sections from Chamber Three to the entrance were partially submerged. Rescuers transported the boys in SKED stretchers through muddy water and over slippery rocks. Initially, the journey took about four to five hours. After a week of draining water and clearance of rocks, it was reduced to under an hour.

For the three mornings of the rescue, Rasmussen and two other divers trudged through a painstaking two-hour trip to their designated positions, training their eyes on the murky water and waiting patiently like eagles ambushing their prey.

At about 2.30 pm on Sunday, a diver emerged, miraculously, holding the first of the boys.

"I was crouching, crawling, walking through water and over rocks, keeping the kids in the stretcher so they could be protected through all of this," said Rasmussen.

For their section of rescue, Rasmussen and his team took 20 minutes to transport the boys on the muddy and steep path. The boys were in cold water for two hours and their core body temperature risked falling to dangerous low levels.

"Time was of the essence for us," he said. "If we fell or were slow it would interrupt not just the flow of what was happening but the whole rescue."

It was a tight passageway from Chamber Three to Chamber Two. Divers piggy-backed the SKED stretcher on a raft and pulled a rope tied to it across chin-deep flood water.

Where there were steep slopes with cascading floods, the stretcher was winched up with a rope pulley system installed at the roof. Where there were low levels of water, pipes, used for pumping out water, were improvised as impromptu slides. In rocky terrain, divers formed a human daisy chain to pass the stretcher in a relay.

"Forty per cent of the rescue route was through the flood water. At least three hours involved diving and moving in water which was up to the rescuers' chests or chins," estimated Rear Admiral Apakorn.

"Was it a casualty or a kid?"

From a distance, when Ivan Karadzic saw the diver approaching with the first boy, he was apprehensive. When he realized the boy was breathing, he heaved a big sigh of relief.

Ivan, a Dane, had moved to Koh Tao a few years after Mikko Paasi. Together, they operated a diving center. Stationed at midpoint, Ivan was responsible for replacing air tanks and guiding rescue divers through. "It was extremely stressful," he recalls, likening it to a disaster zone.

The entire world held its breath as the operation was in progress.

At 5.40 pm Bangkok time, the first boy emerged victoriously from the world's most googled cave. The first rescue took seven hours and 40 minutes. This was followed by a second boy ten to twelve minutes later. The third boy appeared at 7.40 pm followed by the fourth at 7.50 pm. One by one, the Wild Boars were brought out of the darkness of Tham Luang. It was met with mixed emotions. Who was saved? Who were remaining in the cave? Would the rain resume?

To reduce the anxiety of the parents of other boys, the names of the rescued were shrouded in secrecy. It was later learnt, Mark, Tern, Note and Nick were the first four boys rescued.

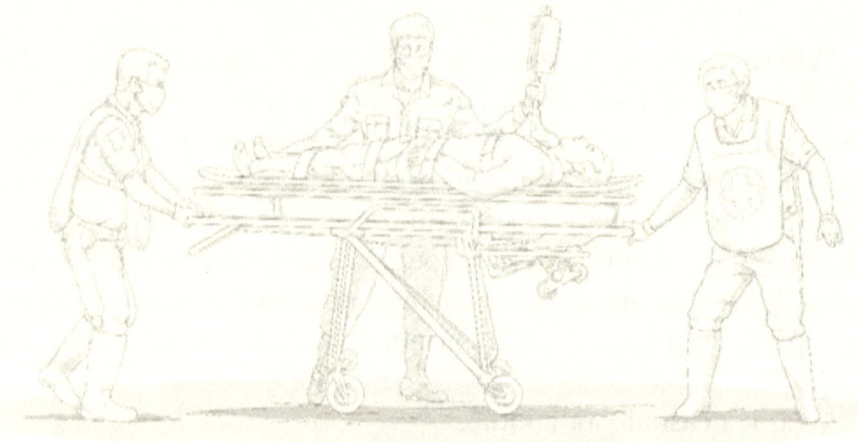

Medic transferring the boy to the waiting ambulances or helicopters

The boys were given oxygen before being transferred to ambulances. Traffic was cleared and roads leading to the hospital were blocked. Thais cheered and applauded loudly as ambulances sped by with sirens wailing to Chiang Rai City. Some of the boys were airlifted by helicopters. It was a momentous occasion many wished to witness first-hand.

"The operation was more successful than expected," beamed a delighted Narongsak.

At the end of the first day of rescue, divers erased their self-doubt harbored initially that the diving option would tank. Now, they were convinced it worked. On the second and third day, the divers were raring to go.

Vern himself expected a "high rate of attrition" in terms of the boys' survival, but his hopes increased after the first day of rescue. "Sunday was when the first four came out and they were all strong and there was nothing really to worry about them. It gave us hope for the next four and the next five," he said, especially after the tragic demise of Saman.

After a short celebration, the divers stayed focused on freeing the remaining boys. They must not be complacent or lower their vigilance.

A successful rescue depended on a reliable supply of oxygen tanks, estimated to be over a hundred, deposited strategically along the passageway. The mission paused overnight for the tanks to be replaced for the operation to resume on Monday and Tuesday.

TIMELINE OF SUNDAY'S RESCUE MISSION

8 am Bangkok time: Areas outside Tham Luang were evacuated for intricate rescue operation. The press area was relocated 1500 feet further down.

10 am: 18 divers - 13 foreign and five Thai - entered the cave.

10.30 am: At the press conference, a spokesman mentioned the main obstacles were time and water. Digging shafts to rescue the boys was ruled out.

10.35 am: Narongsak, head of the rescue operation, announced that rescuers were at "the peak of our readiness". The first boy was projected to emerge around 9 pm. The entire rescue mission was expected to take two to three days.

11.11 am: Thai Navy SEAL posted a photo of linked hands on Facebook and they were ready to bring the Wild Boars football team home.

1 pm. Divers dived from Chamber Three.

1.15 pm: Roads leading to Chiang Rai Prachanukroh Hospital were closed to traffic.

3.30 pm: Thai government posted infographic showing the rescue method - each boy is accompanied by two divers who are guided by ropes. (The plan was since changed)

5.40 pm: First two boys emerged from the cave.

7.05 pm: Tossathep Boonthong, chief of Chiang Rai's health department, announced that two boys were checked at the field hospital outside Tham Luang.

7.20 pm: Two ambulances and a helicopter left for Chiang Rai Prachanukroh Hospital.

7.40 pm: Third boy emerged from cave.

7.50 pm: Fourth boy emerged from cave.

8.50 pm: At the press conference Narongsak confirmed that four boys had been rescued and were in hospital. The second rescue operation was scheduled to begin in the next 10 to 20 hours. This allowed rescuers sufficient time to prepare and replace oxygen tanks.

Rescuers replenishing oxygen tanks

Over three successive days, the rescuers brought out four, four and five survivors, respectively, sticking to the same routine procedures each day. With each rescue, it became more and more efficient, close to perfection.

"If it's not broke, don't change it," Canadian Brown said. "When day one went well, we said - we are going to do the exact same thing on day two."

On the first two days of the rescue, 18 core divers extracted the four boys. On the final day, at least 12 divers took part. Four boys each were extracted on the first two days, and four more boys and their coach on the third day.

Upon hearing the news, Singaporean Douglas Dylan Yeo, 50, a course director in a diving school with 26 years of diving experience, had asked himself, "What do I want to do? What can I do?" Following his heart, Douglas, who was married with two sons, dropped everything and bought a one-way ticket to Chiang Rai. Over the final 70 feet, he crawled on uneven ground with small air pockets before he reached his station. Surviving only on Thai sticky rice, he chanted to achieve calm. Within a team of six divers, he transported the last five boys on SKED stretchers. He could hear the boys breathing heavily. All were asleep except Adul whose eyes were partially open.

A total of ninety divers - 50 foreigners and 40 Thais - were involved in the entire heart-stopping operation. Dr. Harris was one of the last rescuers out of the cave.

JULY 10 – LAST BOY EMERGED

"Fish on!"

The rescuers at Chamber Three signaled when they felt a tug on the rope. It was the sign that the boy, on the eleventh rescue trip, would soon emerge from the flood.

They waited. Fifteen minutes. Thirty minutes. One hour. One hour and a half. No one appeared.

500 feet to Chamber Three, Chris Jewell momentarily released the guide rope to switched the eleventh boy from left to right. Chris made a sweeping motion, with his arms, only to lose his grip of the guide rope. With zero visibility, he could not find it. In four nerve-wracking minutes, he was lost. Instead, he found an electrical cable installed earlier. Chris clenched it, thinking it would lead him to the entrance. Disoriented, Chris dived in the wrong direction.

"I surfaced in a different section of the cave and I really didn't know where I was for several minutes," he said. "I got the boy out of the water, made him comfortable, took off my cave-diving equipment and then I was able to walk around the chamber." Chris and the boy were back at the chamber he had already passed.

Meanwhile, Dr. Harris and Jason were preparing the last boy, Titan, for the dive. He dived to guide two boys out in the past two days.

"The last child is a really small child," Jason said, "The mask didn't fit him. We put it on him, really strapped down tight so his nose was flattened against his face and there was a big gap under his chin. We just couldn't get it to seal."

If his mask didn't secure properly, the boy would drown. There was no way to communicate to other rescuers to bring a new mask. Jason used another mask which had a tighter seal. He pulled the boy close to him and extend his head over so that if they hit a wall, Jason would absorb the impact first. Jason hit the wall a dozen of times but he knew it was a one-way journey and had to move on.

On the way out with the last boy, Dr. Harris and Jason bumped into Chris at the chamber. Dr Harris led the eleventh boy out with Chris following behind. When Dr Harris, Jason and Chris arrived at Chamber Three, they were greeted with thunderous applause from the rescuers.

"When the boys left the cave, obviously, there was a big sigh of relief," said Major Charles Hodges, commander of the US team. "Everyone knew that a big home run had been hit."

"The whole world was watching, so we had to succeed," said Kaew, a Thai Navy SEAL who was amazed at how perfectly the teams labored. "I don't think we had any other choice."

"The last day was the worst day," Vern said. "On the third day you had to get five out, plus four Navy SEALs, and the weather was changing quite rapidly. The water levels did come up on Tuesday. You could see it happening. You could feel the tension."

Drained both physically and emotionally, Vern was still reeling from the success of the rescue.

"Just to get any of them out alive would have been a miracle. But to get 13 out of 13... won't happen again," Vern enthused. "It's the biggest miracle ever."

"I still can't believe it worked," sighed Major-General Chalon chai Chitimacha, deputy commander of the Thai 3rd Army Region, as he shook his head in disbelief. He added, "The most important piece of the rescue was good luck, which helped in the operation. So many things could have gone wrong, but somehow we managed to get the boys out."

"The favorable outcome that has been achieved is almost beyond our imagination when we first became involved," admitted Dr. Harris and Craig, as both Australians expressed relief in rescuing the thirteen without any hitch. Some divers just could not believe it. They had to pinch themselves that they were not in their dreams.

CELEBRATION

Finally, all the boys and their coach were extracted successfully. Residents in the border town of Mae Sai were shedding tears of joy when the news first broke out that all the boys had been rescued.

As soon as John and Rick stepped out of the cave, families hugged and thanked the British heroes profusely.

At 10 pm, four Thai Navy SEALs - one of them was Dr Pak - wearing white masks and sunglasses to protect their identities exited the cave. They gave a thumbs up for a photo shoot. Navy SEALs do not publicize the secretive nature of their work nor seek recognition. They take pride in teamwork. There is no 'I' in a TEAM. There is no room for egoism. Everyone is an equal member of the team. All credit goes to everyone involved in the incredible rescue. The Thai Navy SEALs remain focused and committed to their mission and the force.

Note's aunt, Sarisa Promjak, said. "We don't know how we can ever repay you. If it was possible, I would go down on my knees and bow to each and every one of you."

Hookah! Four Thai Navy SEALS emerged triumphantly

Jubilant villagers lined the roads in Chiang Rai leading to the hospital, applauding the ambulances that sped past. Motorists blared their horns in celebratory mode.

Thai social media was flooded (*no pun intended*) with postings of the rescue that kept the world in suspense. Many posted 'Hookah!' – the signature Thai Navy SEALs shout. 'Hookah!" is the celebratory yell originating from the United States Navy to increase morale, celebrate teamwork and declare affirmation.

All around the world, millions of people who had followed the rescue religiously celebrated the homecoming of the Wild Boars.

PUMP FAILURE

"More water is coming fast! Get out now!"

Kaew heard panicked Australians screaming at the top of their voices. He saw an erratic flight of headlamps rushing toward him as he was about to swallow his last bite of shrimp-and-pineapple pizza. For three punishing days, Kaew and the divers had lifted the thirteen footballers, one by one, through various sections of wet, slippery and craggy rocks. Only moments ago, he congratulated the four-member Navy SEAL team who had accompanied and rescued the boys.

"The boys were safe, and my friends were safe," said Kaew. "I thought, finally, the mission is a success."

The waist-high water suddenly surged threateningly to his chest level. Kaew and twenty other rescuers, without any diving equipment, literally ran for their life – half a mile to the entrance. It was a narrow escape. Everyone panicked and fled.

"If you put your hand in front of you, it just disappeared," described Kaew of the final deluge. "You couldn't see anything."

"All of a sudden a water pipe burst and the main pump stopped working," Ruengrit explained. "We really had to run from Chamber Three to the entrance because the water level was rising very quickly – like two feet every 10 minutes."

At the final moments, Commander Chaiyananta Peeranarong, 60, also heard shouts of alarm. He thought the unprecedented operation, which leaned on the expertise of both elite foreign divers and Thai Navy SEALs, had flipped into a disaster. The former Navy SEAL was among the last to leave the cave.

"By the time the last diver was out, the water was already at head level, almost to the point where he needed an oxygen tank," recalled Chaiyananta. About three hours after the Thai Navy SEALs and last batch of boys emerged from the cave, the entire rescue system suddenly collapsed like a house of cards.

Claus Rasmussen does not have a spiritual explanation, but agrees the timing was eerie. "That everything breaks down as soon as everybody's safe? It's just weird."

"It was like a movie scene, everything was collapsing," Ruengrit said. "It was one of those acts of God. The cave spirit didn't want us in there anymore. It was saying - I've had enough of you guys, it's time to leave."

Only days before, Kaew wrapped his Buddha amulet hanging on his neck in water proof duct tape. He thanked Buddha profusely for saving him, "The cave is sacred. It was protected until the very end."

The fateful evening of July 10 was a wet Tuesday that saw a dramatic closure to a riveting rescue. It had the whole world balancing on a knife-edge. Many villagers in this once-unknown northern Thai town of Mae Sai believed the last-minute flood was an act of the Divine to reclaim its sacred abode. Many believed it was the spirit of Jao Mae Nang Non who closed the cave with a clang, only after all had left.

Call it predestation, synchronicity or divine intervention. In Thailand where the majority are Buddhist, the spiritual transcendence is a vital component of their daily lives.

The cave was now empty again, flooded and inaccessible. In five months, when the dry season begins, workers need to return to collect hundreds of gas tanks and various equipment hurriedly left behind, while cleaners would need to clear up the rubbish at the spiritual cave.

Dr. Harris

Dr. Harris was one of the last rescuers to leave the cave. However, on Wednesday, when the mission had fulfilled its objective, Dr. Harris's father died. It appeared as if he lived to see his son's task being successfully completed. Did the spirit guardian of Tham Luang, Jao Mae Nang Non, have a hand in this?

Asking for privacy, Dr. Andrew Pearce said, "His family's grief was magnified by the physical and emotional demands of the rescue operation. It has been a tumultuous week with highs and lows. Harry is a quiet and kind man who did not think twice about offering his support on this mission."

"He was an integral part of the rescue attempt. He is an extraordinary Australian and he has certainly made a big difference to the rescue effort here in Thailand," said Foreign Affairs Minister Julie Bishop.

"The Australians have been a big help, especially the doctor. Very good. The very best. Without him, this mission may not have succeeded," said the commander of the rescue mission, Narongsak.

Dr. Harris' friend, Sue Crowe painted him as 'an unassuming and selfless family man, whose calm presence would have comforted the boys in the cave. He is brilliant with children, and he would have made sure that they were prepared in the best possible way from a cave-diving perspective. He would have been the perfect person to support them.'

Many Australians requested the government to name him as Australian of the Year - the nation's highest civic honor.

In 2011, Dr. Harris was part of a team that retrieved the body of his friend, Agnes Milowka. During a dive at Tank Cave, South Australia, she ran out of air. The South Australian Government specifically requested for Dr. Harris as the six miles of underwater passageway in the cave was complicated and dangerous.

After two excruciating weeks, the Thai cave boys and their coach emerged nary a scar and were able to see the sun and smell the fresh air again. It was an amazing accomplishment.

The entire jaw-dropping operation was bold, complicated and meticulously planned. Nothing like it had been attempted before. Some of those involved described the risky endeavors undertaken by the expert divers who ferried the boys out, as superhuman. This was history in the making.

This rescue teetering on the brink of a major fiasco – the first of its kind - had the entire world's eyeballs glued to the television and social media. Many had expected the Tham Luang mission to end in tragedy, with at least a few deaths. To the surprise of many, the divers defied all odds. It has become a legendary story of hope, iron will and teamwork.

The whole world saw Narongsak, the commander of the rescue mission, as the hero. He said, "We change mission impossible to mission possible. We did everything that everyone expected us to fail."

Divers of different nationalities brought a repertoire of expert skills acquired internationally - including the ability to install guide lines that aided in low visibility. Cave diving, a form of extreme sports, is rare. It involves the use of specialized equipment, a different set of diving skills and exposure to high risks. Cave rescue divers are even rarer. This tightly-knit kinship of divers worldwide, numbered less than ten.

During the entire operation, the precise mechanics of the rescue were closely guarded. This allowed the rescuers to stay focused and not let the comments of observers to influence their plans. Since then, the cat has been let out of the bag.

For the public who read the newspapers and social media, one Thai Navy SEAL refuted how simplistic the operation looked from the infographics. In reality, it was laden with life-threatening risks. They worked a minimum 12-hour shift and returned to their quarters totally exhausted. Scuba gear, wet towels and boxes of instant noodles were quickly thrown on the floor as they dropped dead-tired into their bunks.

Captain Anan Surawan summed it all up, "We worked until we forgot the time."

HOSPITAL

I t looked like eons since the children went missing. However, at the hospital, the parents could not hug or touch their own offspring right away. The doctors had to quarantine the boys to protect them from cave diseases, e.g. lung infections from bat or bird droppings, dirty water and hypothermia – extreme low body temperature caused by prolonged exposure to water. The parents could only view the boys through the glass panels of the isolation ward. Knowing and seeing their sons alive, however, was good enough. They did not raise any objection to this restriction.

The thirteen rescued underwent a battery of health checks. After two weeks of enclosure and darkness, their eyes were unaccustomed to daylight. Eyeshades were worn initially.

Apart from some minor eye and lung infections, the boys were on the way to the pink of health. They were given antibiotics and appeared to be on the mend.

Finally, the parents were allowed to wear hospital green gowns and masks to meet their beloved *look chaai*, although they had to be separated by six feet. After two weeks of starvation and a few days of liquid diet, the boys were able to savor their favorite foods and desserts again.

A few days later, the doctors declared the boys free of infection. The parents were able to be with their *look chaai* in close proximity again. The conservative Thai culture does not practice the Western form of hugs, kisses and other forms of touchy-feely expressions.

All were recovering at a hospital in northern Thailand's Chiang Rai province, where videos showed several of them in seemingly good spirits, waving and flashing peace signs to the camera. Despite an invitation from FIFA, the Wild Boars were barred from travelling to watch the final of the World Cup.

CONGRATULATORY MESSAGES

Icelandic PM Katrín Jakobsdóttir was the first international leader to rejoice publicly at the news: "Today, hope, compassion, and courage has won. Warmest wishes for a speedy recovery to all of you brave boys from your friends in Iceland."

In his weekly address at St. Peter's Square on Sunday, the Pope spoke about the missing young footballers in Thailand cave. He prayed for the young sportsmen and their wellbeing.

US President Donald Trump was among the first to congratulate Thailand: "On behalf of the United States, congratulations to the Thai Navy SEALs and all on the successful rescue of the 12 boys and their coach from the treacherous cave in Thailand. Such a beautiful moment - all freed, great job!"

From British Prime Minister Theresa May: "Delighted to see the successful rescue of those trapped in the caves in Thailand. The world was watching and will be saluting the bravery of all those involved."

From German Chancellor Angela Merkel: "What wonderful news from Thailand! So much to admire: the perseverance of the brave boys and their coach, the skill and determination of the rescuers."

From Moon Jae-In, President of South Korea: "The Thai boys are now safely back with the families, a miracle made possible by the brave rescue crew, the coach and the boys themselves. I wish them a speedy recovery and remind myself that always, the primary duty of a state is guarding the safety of its people."

From Tshering Tobygay, Prime Minister of Bhutan: "Bhutan celebrates the rescue of the thirteen Wild Boards. Congratulations Thailand! Hookah!"

From Mark Zuckerberg, CEO Facebook: "From everyone at Facebook – your bravery has been amazing and congratulations on the successful rescue of eight Wild Boars. Best of luck as you work to get the remaining three players and their coach to safety."

From tech guru Elon Musk: "Great news that they made it out safely. Congratulations to an outstanding rescue team!" He visited the cave and offered a prototype mini-submarine made from rocket parts. However, the submarine was not needed. Elon left it in Thailand in case it may be useful in the future. He named the submarine, Mu Pa Kruba Boonchum Holy Thread after the revered monk who gave hope to both the families of the boys and the rescuers.

From Chilean miner Mario Sepulveda, who was among 33 miners trapped in a mine for 69 days in 2010: "Youjuuuu! I feel a lot, a lot of emotion. What can I say? I hope these kids will be very successful."

From David Beckham: "So pleased to hear the news from Thailand. These boys are heroes as in the coach, the men and women who risked their lives rescuing them and the incredible Saman Gunan. Such a positive, uplifting story."

From French World Cup Star Paul Pogba dedicated France's World Cup semi-final 1-0 win against Belgium to the 12 boys: "This victory goes to the heroes of the day, well done boys, you are so strong."

From Manchester United: "Our thoughts and prayers are with those affected. We would love to welcome the team from Wild Boars Football Club and their rescuers to Old Trafford this coming season."

EPILOGUE

Before boarding a flight at Chiang Rai, Rear Admiral Apakorn delivered a message to the boys, "Make the most of your lives. Be good people, be a force for good for your country."

The miraculous cave rescue left an indelible mark in the coach and his 12 Wild Boars. Except Adul, all of them shaved their head and got cleansed spiritually in a monastery for nine days as they were ordained as Buddhist novices. Ordaining as a full monk is only available to men over 20.

Entering into monkhood is seen as a way of paying tribute to Saman, who perished while helping to rescue them.

Many of the Wild Boars desire to be either a professional football player and a Navy SEAL when they complete their studies.

Titan testified, "This experience taught me to value my life. This event has made me stronger."

On September 6 at the 'United as One' banquet at the Royal Plaza, Dusit Palace, Adul appropriately summarized the thoughts of the Wild Boars:

"The fact that we have been saved makes us feel that we have to return the gratitude by living good lives, being good children to the parents and being good students to the teachers. After we left the cave, we have learned of the love and care that Thais and people all over the world have for us and we felt overwhelmed and we want to thank you all from the heart."

Come 2118, 100 years from now, many will read Tham Luang miraculous cave rescue with awe just like you read Titanic's maiden voyage on the 100th anniversary of its sinking.

APPENDICES

Main Characters

British Divers
John Volanthen, an IT consultant
Rick Stanton, a former firefighter
Robert Harper
Chris Jewell
Jason Mallinson
Vernon Unsworth, lived near Tham Luang
Bill Whitehouse, Vice-Chair of British Cave Rescue Council

Australian Divers
Dr. Richard Harris, an anesthetist
Craig Challen, a veterinary surgeon

Other Divers
Claus Rasmussen from Denmark
Ivan Karadzic from Denmark

Ben Reymenants from Belgium
Mikko Paasi from Finland
Eric Brown from Canada
Douglas Dylan Yeo from Singapore

Thailand
Narongsak Osottanakorn, Governor of Chiang Rai and Commander
of Rescue Mission
Rear Admiral Apakorn Yuukong-kaew, Thai Navy SEAL commander
Captain Anan Surawan, Commander of the First Special Warfare
Corps, Head of Forward Operating Base at Chamber Three.
Lt. Col. Dr. Pak Loharnshoon, Thai Navy SEAL military medic
Commander Chaiyananta Peeranarong in charge of transfer of
the boys between Chambers Three and Two
Nopparat Khanthavong, head coach of Wild Boars Football Academy
Phra Khuva Boonchum, The Monk of Three Nations
Ruengrit Changkwanyuen, Manager in GM Thailand, coordinator
for the diving teams
Jao Mae Nang Non (The Reclining Goddess)

United States
Major Charles Hodges, commander of the US team

Facts and Figures

12 boys and 1 coach trapped 2.5 miles from Tham Luang entrance.

Total length of Tham Luang: 6 miles.

More than 10,000 rescuers were involved including over 100 divers, 900 police officers, 2,000 soldiers and representatives from about 100 government agencies.

More than 23 countries were involved in rescue.

64 million gallons of water pumped out, equivalent 100 Olympic-sized pools.

More than 700 diving cylinders were supplied.

Distance from Tham Luang to Chiang Rai Prachanukroh Hospital: 38 miles, 1 hour drive.

One fatality, Saman Gunan, a 37-year-old former Thai Navy SEAL

Saturday June 23 2018, 12 boys and their coach entered Tham Luang

Monday July 2 2018, 12 boys and their coach sighted after trapped for 9 days

Sunday July 8 2018, 4 boys rescued after trapped for 15 days.

Monday July 9 2018, the second batch of 4 boys rescued after trapped for 16 days.

Tuesday July 10 2018, final batch of 4 boys and their coach rescued after trapped for 17 days.

THE AUTHOR

Michael Lum, author of *I Once Wore Diapers, Who Broke My Rice Bowl?, From Beggars to Millionaires and Make The World Your Oyster?* lives in Singapore.

He graduated with a Bachelor of Accountancy from National University of Singapore, a Master of Commerce from University of New South Wales and a Master of Professional Education (Training & Development) from Nanyang Technological University.

He is a certified trainer with the American Board of NLP, American Management Association and Center for Body Language. Michael is also a Louis Allen program leader, ICF-certified coach, a Distinguished Toastmaster and Laughter Yoga instructor.

He can be contacted at: MikeLum@HardKnocksCollege.com